MW00879462

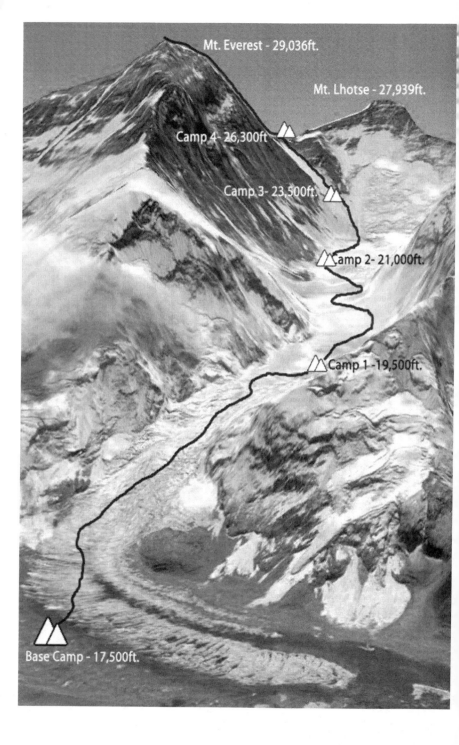

Mt. Everest - 29,036ft.

Mt. Lhotse - 27,939ft.

Camp 4 - 26,300ft

Camp 3 - 23,500ft.

Camp 2 - 21,000ft.

Camp 1 - 19,500ft.

Base Camp - 17,500ft.

Mt. Nuptse - 25,771ft.

Endorsements

"Full of funny and tragic details of the trip, this book is a great look behind the Everest climbing scene and will be informative and inspirational for climbers and non-climbers alike."

Will Cross
world-class mountain climber and motivational speaker,
ascended the highest peaks on all seven continents
and walked to both the North and South Poles

"I was a member of Yury's expedition team, and I summitted Mt. Everest two days after Yury. His book is a gripping and accurate account of the expedition that captures the difficulties, challenges, joys and fears of our great mountain adventure.

Part 3 is a good read for anyone contemplating a high altitude alpine climb since it focuses on what it takes to succeed in this rarefied atmosphere."

Bill Burke

"Climbing Everest without quitting a day job offers an exceptional and deeply personal look into what it takes to climb Mt. Everest. Not only this book is an easy and interesting read, it motivates you to trust your heart and follow your dreams against all odds."

Keith Leon
Book mentor, Speaker & Bestselling Author of the book, Who Do You Think You Are? Discover The Purpose Of Your Life

"This book is not just another book about mountain climbing. From the first chapter till the very end, See it from the Top presents great story telling. It is a detailed, day-by-day account that is sometimes unnerving and sometimes very funny. This is also a book with many careful medical observations and technical improvements that could be useful in sport medicine.

Fast-paced and easy to read, Yury's story is a great inspiration for anyone who loves challenge, self-improvement and adventure."

Alexander Golbin, M.D., Ph.D.
Medical Director Sleep and Behavior Medicine Institute Editor in Chief: Sleep and Health journal

"Climbing to the top of the world is as much a psychological battle as much as it is a physical effort. I am sure all the readers will greatly enjoy this book and treasure it as a resource as they plan their own expeditions."

Ang Tshering Sherpa
Immediate Past President, Nepal Mountaineering Association. Chairman, Asian Trekking

"How to climb Everest without quitting your day job is one of the best stories of an ordinary person reaching his unordinary dream."

Apa Sherpa
Word record holder, 21 Everest Summits

"A highly emotional book written by a strong man. It shows what it takes to make it to the top. The book reads in one sitting, it captures you, and through it you see a different world described with talent and passion."

Dr. Mark Dykman,
Professor of Physics, Michigan State University

"Yury is an immensely practical thinker, and the engineer in him is clear to see in this great book. He analyses and explains in detail the step by step process that took him to the summit of Mt. Everest. I call Yury "the Rocket" because of his strength, determination and speed in climbing. I am proud to have played a small part in Yury's great success."

Dawa Steven Sherpa
Leader, Eco Everest Expedition, Managing Director, Asian
Trekking

SEE IT FROM THE TOP

How to Climb Everest Without Quitting
Your Day Job

Yury Pritzker

CHICAGO

See it From the Top.
How to Climb Everest Without Quitting Your Day Job

Copyright © 2012 by Yury Pritzker

All rights reserved. No part of this book may be reprinted or transmitted in any form or by any means without a written permission of the author. Please e-mail with your requests at ypritzke@yahoo.com

`

Cover design by John Grantner and Yury Pritzker
All pictures by Yury Pritzker
Part 4 is written by Svetlana Pritzker

Book's web site: www.seeitfromthetop.com
Yury Pritzker's web site: www.himalayasdream.com

ISBN–13   978-1467906456
ISBN–10   146790645X

To my lovely wife, who gave me the strength, courage and wisdom to *see it from the top,* and to my whole family who survived this experience

CONTENTS

Prologue

The Dream

I am brewing my water from snow and chunks of ice. I am in my tent in Camp 3, but it does not seem real. The tent is much larger than usual and somehow I do not see the opposite wall of it; but it does not bother me. I am fully dressed with my backpack ready. I am cross-checking all the gear that I need for the day against the list of the summit gear that I carry with me. It was strategically positioned in my down suit pocket back home in Chicago. I am ready to go, but I am not moving. I do not know why, but something is holding me back...

The next thing I remember is I am sliding my ascender along the rope and moving up. It feels like I am moving in slow motion. I see myself climbing from a distance and I remember that this is how people describe out-of-body experiences. Looks good to me –

the guy there is struggling and I am just watching. One step – four breaths, another step – another four breaths.

I am alone. I do not see anyone in front of me or behind me. Where is the famous traffic jam on the Everest slopes? The sun is shining and reflects off of the blue ice of Lhotse face. The whole face is pure ice. Where is the snow? Was it windy before so all the snow disappeared? I do not remember. It is exceptionally calm now…

It is very early morning and it looks like I am still climbing the Lhotse face. I know that for sure, but I see the tents of Camp 4 on the South Col way down. How come I passed Camp 4 from Camp 3 without stopping there? I do not remember nor do I care. The tents look very colorful on this landscape of black and white. I stop to take in the view.

I do not feel tired. It is a strange feeling because I actually do not feel my body. I am very comfortable – not too cold, and not too hot. I am still climbing in the solitude and now approaching the Balcony. It is a very small place and I am not stopping there – I continue climbing up.

Time disappears into nonexistence; it is limitless yet this fact has no significance to me at the moment. I am not in a hurry to reach the summit, just moving along.

Here is the Hillary Step. Many ropes hang down from the top and I am clipping myself to one of them. I am using the front points of my crampons to climb it, no problem. I look down from the top to where I came from and see the South Summit. Well, I do not remember passing it. How did that happen? It does not matter now. I will visit it on the way down.

All of a sudden I am on the summit ridge. Again, I see the summit not from my position on the ridge, but from the summit itself. I see myself approaching it. I am looking exactly like some people I have seen in pictures; it's somehow funny to me. The summit is very close – one hundred yards away, maybe more. But it looks like I have been moving for hours and it is still in front of me. Finally I am taking my last step.

I am there! I can see in all directions and everything is below me. I am in an exhilarating state. All is possible now. I am turning my face toward the sun, trying to reach it warmth. I do not feel it. The sun is very strong. My eyes are closed and I am trying to open them. But they are very heavy.

Using all my will I am opening my eyes slowly, still holding on to this feeling of victory and space. The sun is shining from my bedroom windows directly on my face. I just climbed Everest in my dream, again, and it feels wonderful. I am now probably holding the world record of the most Everest Summits climbed in dreams. It should count for something.

I am fully awakened now, but the feeling and vibrations of the achievement are buzzing all over my body. Today is Sunday, and I am lying in my bed, enjoying the sun. As my brain returns from the climb back to the reality, a myriad of thoughts are going through it. Most of them are considering and reconsidering the decision that I have to make. I cannot quiet it down: my logical mind argues with me all the time.

So… Do you want to see the Himalayas?

Of course I want to see the Himalayas, all these

famous peaks that I read and dreamed so much about. At least to see them once in my life.

Just to see? Or climb?

Climb? Sure I want to climb there. But can I? Why not? I climbed Denali.

You are crazy. Are you sure about this? Do you think you are ready?

No, I am probably not ready; but I am running out of time.

Yes, this is a great excuse. You have to use it. So what do you want to climb there – Everest?

I am thinking about 8000m peaks. Which one? Of course it is not Everest with my experience, but I still want to see it – that is given. Lhotse is a good one. It is close to Everest, 4th highest in the world and technically challenging. I also want to see Khumbu Icefall. The way to Lhotse goes through it and it's almost identical to Everest. In addition, Lhotse option is relatively inexpensive in comparison to Everest.

So it will be Lhotse. I am going to be living in the Everest Base Camp with all the Everest climbers. I will be going through the Khumbu Icefall and I will be climbing the 4th highest peak in the world that is even more technically difficult then Everest.

Is that all you want?

No, I want Everest. But it is much more expensive and 400m higher. These 400m can make a huge difference. And what if I get sick at 7500m? Should I spend that much money on Everest and risk getting sick at the same place as if would be climbing Lhotse? No, it does not make sense. I will go with Lhotse first and if all goes well next time I will go for Everest.

Ha! Who is giving you the money and that much time from work to do two expeditions?

Ok, then it is just one expedition. I am 53; I am running out of time. Can I be fit to climb at my age? Statistics do not support it. If it is only one expedition, then it has to be Mt. Everest.

What is better – to fail at Everest or to succeed on Lhotse?

Good point. It is better to climb Lhotse. Right, let's do Lhotse.

What if you fail on Lhotse?

Possible, but less embarrassing.

Embarrassing? But who is going to judge?

Everyone.

Are you climbing these mountains to be a hero?

No, no, no… maybe a little…no, no, back off. I am climbing to see the Himalayas. I am climbing because I like climbing. I want to experience this adventure.

And you want others to see how cool you are, right?

Well, it's a complex feeling; not one or the other. But honestly, no! I want to climb it because I want to climb!

So what is it going to be: Lhotse or Everest?

Can I do both? Why not?!

You are not sure you can do either of them, now you are talking about doing both? – Real HERO!!!

Yes, I want to be a hero. What is wrong with being a hero?

Nothing is wrong, just admit it.

Okay. Yes, I want to be a hero.

Well, at least we know that one for sure. Where do you get the money for all of these? Do you have money for Lhotse?

I can get money. I can borrow.

Let's leave money for now. What do you really want?

I don't know… I don't know. I want to climb.

Let's start from the beginning. Do you want to go to Himalayas?

Yes. Yes.

Do you want to see Everest?

Yes.

There are only 2 choices: Lhotse, or Everest. Which is it going to be?

Okay, let's come back to the idea of climbing both. The route is the same. It is just a small deviation after Camp 3, so it might not be twice as expensive.

Good. Now, we are getting somewhere.

Here is what I'm going to do. I will arrange for both expeditions, pay only extra for Lhotse permit and decide what to do on the mountain. If I do not feel well enough at Camp 3, I am going to Lhotse. If I feel strong, I am going for Everest.

You are a genius! That is brilliant – just a little more money than Everest requires. Hah, just a minute ago you were not sure how to pay for Everest at all.

Forget about the money. I will get the money. I will figure something out.

Well. I'll tell you what. You are not going to do any of these. You will fail everywhere. You do not have it clear in your head. You cannot get there with this level of thinking: "If I feel well, this will happen, if I do not feel well, this will happen…." This is just a recipe for disaster. Set your goals. Visualize them. Trust yourself. Go for it!

Of course you are right. Okay. Done. I am going for Everest. I will climb Everest. I will get money for

Everest. I am already there – on top of the world. I just climbed Everest! And it feels wonderful!

Part 1 – The Beginning

August 1967 – Wow!!!

I am dying of thirst. I don't know why we do not have water with us. I think I have never been this thirsty in my life, but it does not matter. What I see in front of me is a dream world that is coming from the stories that I have read or from my imagination. It does not seem real, as beautiful and calm as it is. The sky is dark blue and the clouds are forming huge figures that cover the mountain range. I am in awe of the glaciers and peaks that are in front of me. I can hear people talking, but I am not listening.

I am scanning the range from right to left and back, peering into the little details and cannot understand how it is possible to create all of this. It is very hot and little bees are buzzing, working hard on a beautiful meadow spread on the wide top of the peak where we are sitting

This is how I remember my first climb during my

visit to the mountains in 1967. I was twelve years old then. My parents took me and my sister – who was only four years old at the time – to our first big trip to Caucasus Mountains.

My first climb in Caucasus Mountains

It was a remarkable journey for my family. We were living in Russia at the time. My dad had a small car and we drove 1500km from Kiev where we lived to Dombay, a now very famous area of the Caucasus Mountains. I remember that it took us three days of driving on narrow, badly maintained roads, but it was worth it. We were accompanied by two couples: my dad's friends, who were driving their bikes all that way with us. At that time the Dombay area was not developed at all and we had to spend a week living in tents. My dad's friends were experienced alpinists and I managed to follow them on some of their hikes.

One day we went to the Alibek glacier and I remember the deep silence and stillness of the mountains disturbed only by light cracks of the glacier. At some point, one of the ladies called loudly to her husband who was climbing the side moraine of the glacier. Her high pitched voice broke the silence and two stones came down from the moraine top, rolling toward us. Their dash down disturbed the silence only for a short time and then the stillness of the void came back. There was something magnificent in this serenity, a feeling that I had never experienced before. I still get chills remembering it.

The beauty I saw that day changed my life forever. Together with my dad's friends, who were much younger than he was, I climbed my first peak. As I said before, we did not have any water out there, but nevertheless I remember a sense of achievement, confidence and freedom that I experienced sitting on the top of that peak.

After this first encounter I went to different mountaineering trips multiple times with my friends, but in 1975 I got my first real adventure. I was a university student at the time and managed to get into the mountain camp of the neighboring university. I still had no idea what it took to climb the mountains, but I was ready and willing to learn. At the camp they split all of us in a few different groups according to our experiences. Because I was not a student at the university, I got into the mishmash group of outsiders and ended up with the more experienced climbers.

It was an amazing experience for me. I worked with ropes, crampons and many other advanced techniques. I remember taking each day at a time, not even questioning or knowing what was going to happen the next day. Just taking it all in.

From 1975 until 1989, when my family immigrated to the United States, I participated in many climbing expeditions, mostly in my beloved Caucasus Mountains. Eventually I gained enough experience to lead others on multiple climbing trips. In 1981 I even had the guts to take my wife on our honeymoon trip to the mountains. We were accompanied by a bunch of our friends who did not have any experience as well. Later many of these friends joined different mountain clubs and went climbing on their own.

It was almost impossible to buy any climbing equipment at this time in Russia. Russian climbers used a system of alpinists' camps where people could meet and arrange to climb together. This series of camps were supported by the government and if you were part of this system, you could get some rental equipment during your camp participation. The rest of us were out of the system and on our own.

Most parties like ours ended up making their own equipment. I learned how to sew using my grandma's foot powered Singer sewing machine and began making my own equipment, the first of which were two very light tents made out of parachute material. I ended up creating windbreakers and even warm insulated parkas. It was very difficult to obtain my supplies – used military parachutes that were sold on occasion only in one store in Kiev. I would often go there and stand in long lines just to see if the fabric was even available. The parachute fabric was great for protecting against wind, but it was easily penetrated by the rain or snow. So, we needed to make plastic covers to protect it. This plastic cover would need to be reinforced at the corners where runners would be attached to avoid damage. This huge plastic construction and reinforcement was created by using a hot iron and two strips of foil that would allow the ironing plastic sheets to stay together without melting. Unfortunately, such covers did not have the right shape as modern tent covers do. They would flip constantly against the tent with the wind, producing thunderstorm like sounds during the night.

One of the major problems was the transportation of fuel for our camp stoves. We used plastic shampoo bottles that were difficult, if not impossible, to find. They were the best and almost the only choice for our purpose. One of the disadvantages of such "equipment" was that all of them were leaky. The smell of the gasoline was following us all the time, penetrating our food supplies and clothes. Some people invented a very complicated method of carrying their fuel using empty cans from canned food. They would buy liquid based canned food, make a small cut, get food out, and clean it. Then they would fill it with gasoline and use a hot iron to fuse the hole closed.

Imagine my amazement and excitement about the western civilization advancement in this area that I discovered during our immigration to the US. I found empty plastic Coke bottles available everywhere. These plastic containers were much better and did not leak. So, my first thought was to send them back to my friends in Russia.

Another problem was that the clothes that we had been wearing in the mountains were mostly made out of cotton that now is considered to be a "death" fabric for climbers. It was very common to get to your tent after a long hard day of climbing with your undershirt all wet from sweat, change into a dry spare one for the night and in the morning find that the wet one is completely frozen. You would still need to change back into the wet one to start climbing as you would normally carry only one spare t-shirt, for the night. The cotton t-shirts could not dry during the walking days, so the only time we had a chance to dry them was during rest days.

In 1979, I developed a problem with my right knee. I did not know what had happened, but it was swollen and I was running a fever. I remember seeing every possible doctor in Kiev, but no one could diagnose the problem. Finally, they decided to put me into a cast and start treating me with all sorts of antibiotics. I spent six months in the hospital with that cast. My right leg became bone thin and the swelling of my knee was gone, together with the rest of my muscles. I spent another three months in rehabilitation and managed to gain some of my muscle mass and strength back.

When I asked my doctor when I could return to climbing, he told me that I should be grateful that I could walk. According to his opinion, climbing was out of the question. I apparently did not take his advice seriously because two months after I left rehab I went skiing. I really could not ski as the way I could before, because my leg was very weak and I was in pain every time I stepped on it. I was afraid that I could not get down all the way from a single long ski run, so I decided to control my distances by not using the ski lift. I would climb up for a short distance and then ski back down, and then climb up again sometimes gaining a little more altitude.

The next summer I was strong enough to get back to climbing. Even today, thirty years after that accident my right leg is still thinner than the left one. After all these years I still felt some pain, in this leg while coming up or down until probably five years ago, when I started training on the Stair Master. I was pleasantly surprised that the side effect of this training: my right knee stopped hurting.

In 1988 my best friend and I went together to the Caucasus Mountains again. I thought this would be my last mountain adventure. I knew that I was moving into the unknown, immigrating to my new country, and climbing was not my immediate priority or even a part of my imagination. I was concerned with surviving, learning the language, and finding a job. I needed to find a way to support my family – we already had two small children ages seven and four.

The four of us came to the United States in 1989 with $500 and four suitcases. It took us some time to get on our feet, and get some decent jobs before thinking about any hobbies like climbing. But the mountains were always on my mind.

We chose mountains for most of our family vacations. Every year we would spend a week in Colorado, skiing – all my family members are expert skiers. My wife can also snowboard, so we even used to carry double equipment for her.

At the ages of 7 and 10 years old we took our kids to Long Peak where we started climbing at two o'clock in the morning and met the sunrise way above the tree line. We could not reach the summit, because the kids were still too young, but it was an interesting experience for all of us. I believe they will remember it forever.

Another time I took the whole family for two days of climbing up to Colorado at the 14,000 foot peak. We carried food, a tent and all the necessary equipment. My daughter was only 12 and she did not like the challenge. I believe it was a turning point for her when she decided not to climb with me anymore. It was different for my son though. When he was 17 he asked me if we can do some real climbing. I praise him now as he renewed my desire for climbing.

We went to the climbing school together and spent six days learning how to climb challenging routes in the Cascade Mountains. We loved every minute of it. I still remember very clearly what a mess we made in our tent, how we could not find our stuff, and many other moments that made our first experience in climbing together so much fun. My son and I still climb together sometimes. He is now more interested in rock climbing and I am hooked on mountaineering... again!

It took me quite a while to understand what had changed in equipment and climbing over the years before I could participate in my first training climb. What I discovered once I got through school was another problem: I had to switch from having no choice back in Russia to having multiple choices here in America. Every single piece of equipment and clothing existed and could be purchased in hundreds of varieties. Well, it took me seven years and a climb to the top of Mt. Everest to be able to say that I now know what to take with me on a climb.

April 2006 – Cold Feet

I do not feel my toes. I can still move them, but I do not feel them.

Is this how people lose their toes?

What should I do?

Just as my wife taught me before this trip, I am using my imagination, sending warmth to my feet, moving them all the time. But I also have to pay close attention to what is going on. We are coming down from the West Ridge of Mt. Hunter in Alaska after a long, long day.

The snow storms that frequently followed us on this climb did not allow us to proceed as planned. We had an avalanche threat every day. So, we stayed at the lower camps, trying to see if the weather would give us any breaks. When we had only three days left before our scheduled flight back from the Kahiltna Glacier, we were able to climb up to the high camp at the beginning of the West Ridge.

It was around 11:00 a.m. when we reached the high camp location after climbing for five hours. Then Greg suggested going to the summit right away, instead of climbing up the next day as we planned. It was a good idea as we all felt pressed for time and were not sure about the next day's weather. It was very light at night this time of the year, so we could climb all night if we needed to. We all voted for it!

We spent an hour digging platforms for our tents, and then another hour eating and drinking. The views from our spot on the ridge were spectacular and I felt that I could draw this view with my eyes closed as I was so familiar with it. The route to this point was on the same side of Mt. Hunter where we were climbing, gaining more and more altitude from camp to camp. Mt. Foraker was in front of us and we could see Mt. Denali (McKinley) on the right. These two Alaskan giants were so magnificent that I caught myself moving my eyes from one mountain to another, all day long, day after day.

So, we are on the move again, going up along the West Ridge. There are five of us. Greg is leading the way and we are following. The route is pretty difficult technically as it requires traversing the icy spans of the ridge by going up and down using the front points of our crampons. We are constantly bypassing huge icy seracs and sometimes have to go far to the left side of the ridge and down in order to avoid walking on top of huge hanging cornices that are making our route pretty unsafe. We are progressing slowly because not all of us are comfortable with these front pointing traverses. Around 8 pm we stop and Greg takes out his radio to listen to the weather forecast. It is going to be clear, but the temperature at the summit will be around -25°F that night.

We discuss our options. Greg asks each of us if we are ready for climbing in this extreme temperature as we would need to climb all night to get up to the summit and come down to the camp. He does not insist on returning, but he also does not encourage us to go on. He wants us to make the right decision for ourselves. It is probably around -15°F now and I am wearing my large down parka even on the way up. I feel good and want to continue, but everyone does not share my mood... we are turning around.

It takes us many hours to get down to the camp as now we need to negotiate the same difficult traverses going down in the deceiving Alaskan night light.

It is almost three in the morning as we reach our tents. I am in a hurry to take off my boots to see the damage. To my surprise and delight, nothing has happened. My toes are coming back alive pretty quickly. I'm happy that all of the challenges are behind us, but thoughts about not being able to get to the top are creeping in.

We are drinking water and discussing our plans before going to sleep. My idea is to try to go to the summit again in the morning. Greg is OK to accompany me, but the rest of the company decides that last night's adventure was enough for them. There is one thing we need to consider: if we go for another attempt in the morning, we would need to get back down to the camp no later than 8pm and start going down to the Kahiltna glacier right away that night. We need to avoid coming down during the daytime when the avalanche danger is much greater.

I feel confused. I believe that I have enough strength to try for the summit once more in the morning, but the lack of climbing experience in such low temperature scares me too. So, I am indecisive. Looking back, I think that it was a mistake to make a decision just after we came back from such an exhausting day. After a couple of hours of sleep I would probably have felt rested and we would have seen everything with fresh eyes. But at that moment I could not withstand the peer pressure and decided to get down with everyone.

In the morning the sun is much stronger than we have observed so far. It is too dangerous to go down right away and we have to stay the whole day in the camp waiting for the cold to take over the steep snow slopes and freeze them to protect us from avalanches.

I am scanning the view in front of me again and focusing on Denali. Its enormous West Face is not that scary any more, after yesterday. I know that there are seven thousand vertical feet that separates me from its summit, but it does not seem to be a problem now.

How does the route go on Denali?

Greg shows us the normal route, the West Rib Route, and the Casing Ridge route.

I want to go there. I definitely want to go there.

We are starting our descent at 9:00 p.m. All is going well. At some point we are crossing the traces of a very fresh avalanche and we are so glad that we were patient enough to wait the whole day before coming down. We come to the Kahiltna glacier around four in the morning, tired, but glad that all we've been through is over. We can get a couple of hours of rest before our last walk to Base Camp with the lending strip. It is just a couple of miles away.

We do not put up our tents and just use them to cover the snow. We are lying on top of them in our sleeping bags. It is a little cold, but the sleep takes over and I am climbing Denali in my dream…

May 2007 – Mt. Denali, Alaska

I am basically buried in the snow. I do not know if I still have my skis on or not. I definitely still have my backpack and it pulls me down deep. My goggles, mouth and everything else is packed with snow. How do I get up?

I make another attempt to stand up, but fall over again on this very steep terrain and sink even more. Greg yells, encouraging me to get up and move faster as we are on the avalanche prone slope. We need to move. Finally I manage to stand up in this virgin powder with my skis still on and 50 lbs. on my shoulders. I am cleaning my goggles and getting ready to start our crazy ski descent. Crazy because not only do we ski down on a steep powder slope with fully loaded backpacks but also because three of us are roped up with me, the lucky one, being in the middle of the rope.

We are descending from the 16,300 foot high West Rib camp of Denali to the 14,200 ft. camp that is now visible down below the slope. I just hope that we are far enough from Base Camp, that observers can't see my struggles. I feel embarrassed, which makes me even more nervous.

I am a good skier. I proved this many times skiing the normal route (the Denali route that most people take) while waiting for better weather and killing time at the 14,200 ft. camp. But this type of descent is something I have never experienced before. I have never skied roped up in the deep powder where three of us had to move in synchronized fashion with our heavy backpacks. My skis are not as wide as the other two guy's skis and I sink deeper into the powder – at least this is how I explain to myself why I fall more often than they. As the decent progresses, we make more and more accurate turns, but we still have to stop frequently as the altitude takes our breath away. Finally we slide into the camp and get to our tents that are located on the opposite side of the camp.

Denali Summit, 2007

Yesterday, we reached the top of Mt. Denali. It was an amazing feeling after so many days of bad weather. We stayed on the summit for a very short time because the wind started blowing stronger and stronger. The storm caught up to us just thirty minutes into the descent, very soon after we reached the Football Field – the large flat area near the summit, and continued punishing us all the way down. We were very tired and gotten to the tents almost at midnight. Some of the guys got small frostbites on their faces, but I was fine. I was wearing my Psolar mask and goggles that behaved well – they did not fog up on me.

In the beginning, our expedition started very well. We managed to carry all the supplies that were split between our backpacks and sleds without double carrying them almost to the 14,200 ft. camp. Normally, all teams do "double carry" which means that they split their weight load into two portions, carry one portion up during the first day, then once they reach the next camp location and unload, they go down, spend the night at the lower camp, and carry up the rest of the stuff the next day. They reach the higher camp with the second portion of the supplies and spend another night there. This helps their acclimatization and relieves people from carrying up too much weight at the same time. Our team felt strong and we managed to carry everything at once.

The other unique feature of our team is that we all travel on skis instead of snowshoes as most of the teams do on Denali. It allows us to move faster and I believe more safely. We use back country type skis that are specially designed to go up, using "skins" or special fabric that we attach to the sliding surface of the skis. This fabric does not allow the skis to slide down, but permits them to move up easily. Bindings of such skis allow one's heels to move up and down similar to the cross country skis. On the way down we snap the back of the bindings into the alpine position, remove the skins and off we go, skiing down like downhill skiers.

On the more steep sections we either go up zigzagging or sometimes attach ski crampons, the metal pieces that hold our skis on icy slopes. At the 25-30 degree slope we have to take skis off and carry them attached to the backpacks. In these sections we are much heavier than other climbers on snowshoes because of the weight of our skis and bindings.

Denali; carrying loads

The weather was almost perfect, so we reached 14,200ft. camp in five days. This camp is a very famous place were all climbers gather to get good acclimatization and wait for the appropriate weather to start their summit push. There are multiple routes leading from this camp to the summit. The normal route that most people take is considered the easiest to the summit. It goes via the so called head wall – a pretty steep section that ends at the ridge where the "high" camp is built. Another route that our team plans to take is the Upper West Rib route. Here we would also need to build our high camp but on a very narrow shelf on the West Ridge.

Because the 14,200 foot camp is the base for acclimatization, most teams spend a lot of time there which gives everyone time to talk, to meet many climbers that came from all over the world, and get to know each other. By my estimate we had around 150 people who were there at the time.

After a couple of days in the camp the weather conditions changed and our problems started. For the whole twelve days the summit wind was around 50 – 60 mph and the temperature was predicted to be between -25° and -30°F. In addition, we had fresh snow almost every day, so the 5 foot high snow wall that we built on the first day was buried completely. Denali was un-climbable. Most of the teams were smart enough not to even try to get to their high camp. However some teams did not have any more patience for waiting at 14,200ft. camp and went to the upper camps just to discover that not only they could not go to the summit, but they could not even leave the tent to go to the bathroom. Yes, this is what was happening up there. They all managed to get down to the 14,200 ft. camp were the wind was not as strong and the weather was not that bad. Most of them went down to fly home.

Interesting to note how the bathroom problem is solved in Denali 14,200ft. camp. You can imagine that such a problem can be really challenging having so many people in one relatively flat large place which is completely covered with snow.

There are actually Denali National Park rangers

living in this camp. Their role is to help climbers in case of emergencies and make sure that all is going according to the rules and regulations of the park. They also maintain two toilets. Both of them have a deep hole that is dug out in the ice. One has three short walls made out of plywood with a fourth being an opening that allows people to get in and out. The height of the walls barely covers your butt when you stand. This toilet does not have a lot of fans as it requires you to squat.

Toilet at 14,200 ft. camp on Denali

The second toilet is a real beauty. That is why, I think, it is placed almost in the middle of the camp. It has a real toilet. Yes, a real ceramic toilet! However to compensate and make the camp an equal opportunity poop camp (EOPC) it does not have plywood walls – just some little walls that are made out of snow and ice bricks. These bricks are very common construction materials on Denali because the snow is very compressed and easy to cut with the special snow saw that almost every team carries. Anyway, these walls surround this toilet like a spiral, protecting it from all directions. For the same equality reasons they are not higher than the wooden ones.

Because of the ceramic toilet's height, people are sitting there visible to everyone in the camp. I see at least two reasons for such design. First, it makes the person sitting inside look like a king or a queen sitting on a throne. Second, it allows other people to be jealous of them because it is not that easy to become a king or a queen. As I mentioned the popularity of this toilet is very high and usually there is a long line standing along these little walls. People in the line are usually very friendly and to suppress the call of nature, are preoccupied in conversations that sometimes involve people sitting on the throne. I was personally a witness of such engaging conversation between one lady sitting on the toilet and the first man in line. They discussed the usual things in such situations: weather, food, etc. When the lady was preparing the last action before putting her pants up the man decided to be a real gentleman and introduced himself. They apparently were not acquainted before.

Back to the climb. We were patient but that was not easy. It was my first real experience with such a large expedition where the wait period is equal or even longer than the climbing part. These were the tests that I was conducting with myself, mostly unconsciously. Can I withstand the cold and be patient? This is what it would take to go on to Himalayas. It was not clear yet in my mind, but I knew that I would have had to have at least these two qualities before allowing myself to dream about the highest mountain. We had to go home soon. We were running out time.

Finally Greg's intuition allowed us to spring into action. Even though our morning team meeting ended with the decision to wait for another day, the wind had suddenly stopped around noon. Greg decided to go to the upper camp at 16,300 feet and make a summit attempt next. We were ready in an hour.

A day before, two Korean climbers lost their patience and made an attempt to get to high camp at 16,300 feet on the West Rib of Denali, which took them eight hours instead of three or four. They did not use skis, instead they climbed on foot, moving very slowly in fresh deep snow that almost reached their waist. The West Rib route was very unsafe because of the huge amount of fresh snow and the corresponding avalanche danger. We were observing their progress the whole day and prayed for their safety. After reaching the high camp they were not only very exhausted, but also found the tent that they left a week before destroyed by the storm. They had to abort their summit attempt that they were planning for the following day.

However, their heroic efforts gave us some confidence that we can still take the initially planned West Rib route. We actually had to consider the normal route by now as the West Rib route was so unsafe. No team had yet climbed the West Rib in that season. It is usually considered to be more difficult and was definitely more dangerous that year because of the weather.

Our plan was to climb on skis
and then switch into climbing boc
push the next day. Our first roped tri
I reached the camp in three hours. V
our cache and preparing platforms fo
was a lot of work, digging and shoveli
being at this altitude really did not help. ⸺ ₊₊ ₁eet I
could only shovel for a minute and then needed to rest
for a minute. Our second roped group was an hour and
a half behind us and we managed to get the two
platforms almost done before they came in. The evening
was beautiful and calm, and we were enjoying the view
from this unique place, perched on our two tiny
platforms on the West Rib.

In the tent on Mt. Denali

The summit day was not all that difficult for me. I
just needed to adjust to the slow pace at this altitude.
We climbed so slowly (or at least it seemed that way to

at I found myself being a little bit annoyed with long breaks. Later I realized that you cannot rush at these altitudes and have to pace yourself. After the famous Football Field, the huge flat space after the West Rib route meets the normal route, you can see the summit and the last span of the climb that looks like a ski slope at the ski resort. It was a little disappointing that there was no ski lift there at this time.

We slowly negotiated the slope on foot. The summit ridge was narrow and long. The wind picked up significantly, carrying the snow powder almost horizontally and hitting us in the face. Our climbing rope also tried to fly away. It picked up from the ground reassembling itself into a horizontal position. We had a couple of hundred yards left and we were on the summit.

As I lay on my back, peering in to the sky at the 14,200 ft. camp, I remember the last two days. There are only a couple of hours left before we go back down to the landing strip on the Kahiltna Glacier for our flight back home. Unfortunately, we cannot stay here and rest for another day – no more time left and most of us have to get back to work. At this time of the year it is too dangerous to go down during the day time. The sun melts the glacier and the snow bridges that span across crevasses might be too weak to hold our weight. We have to go down at night when the temperature freezes the bridges and get to Base Camp before the next morning.

We are all tied into one very long rope: six people and six sleds going down. I thought it would be fun to go down on skis, just skiing downhill on the not very steep glacier. This turned out not to be the case. The descent is extremely painful and unpleasant though we are covering a great distance very rapidly. The rule is to keep the rope tight and in order to do so, everyone has to follow the speed of the leader. We are all in the "pizza" skiing position. Our skis are sliding down the narrow snow road indented with thousands of frozen steps created by people going back and forth on a glacier. With all this weight, our thighs are burning and we can hold the line of descent maybe a minute or two until someone screams: "Stop". We all stop, have a little rest and descent continues.

It is very late at night now. It is still relatively light, yet very foggy. We are not moving fast anymore because the glacier is almost flat. The whole path is marked, but these marks are pretty far from each other and in this lighting conditions and fog we cannot see the next mark most of the time. There are some other teams behind us, following in our steps. It is safe to have someone in front of you, so you can see where they managed to go through without falling into crevasses. There is only one guy in front of us and it is very weird. He is not supposed to be here alone and un-roped because it is the most dangerous part of the glacier. But he is in front of us, looking for the safe path through and we are gratefully following him.

Suddenly the rope tightens and Fred who was in front of me, leading, disappears into a crevasse. I am instinctively in the belay position and holding the fall. Everyone freezes in place. No one moves. Not the guy in front of us nor the people behind. Everyone understands what is going on.

We drag Fred back to the surface. Fortunately he is fine, just a bit scared. How come Fred fell into the crevasse being on skis following this single guy who just safely went through this place? The guy in front does not move any more. He silently waits for us to bypass him and then starts following us. This is good.

The base camp of Mt. Denali is full of tents. People did not fly out last night because of the weather and there is little hope for the flight today. The small four seater planes that fly here can only land with clear visibility. We are taking pictures and drinking frozen beer that Greg has saved for the occasion. I am thinking of what is next. Himalayas seems to be the logical choice...

September 2008 – To Climb or not to Climb?

A m I ready as a climber to try Mt. Everest?

What am I going to wear at the summit day?

Do I need new crampons?

People are saying that 0°F sleeping bag is good for Camp 4. Is my old bag still good enough?

Will I have courage and be able not to lose perspective in life and to turn back at any point of the climb if needed?

What is going to happen if I do not reach the top?

Will I feel humiliated, disappointed, destroyed…?

Do I bring my own food?

What company am I going with?

How do they survive here at home without me for two months?

How do I recognize that I have pulmonary or cerebral edema?

Do I buy new boots?...

These questions flood my mind in a matter of seconds. All these thoughts coming and going in random order again and again. It is difficult to make such a huge decision that affects so many aspects of one's life and not to be overwhelmed by the details. I know that details can make me fail at this stage even before I commit to the expedition. I am reading books, and other people's blogs, and details of the expedition are piling up. I have to first make a decision about going and then dive into the details. But how can I see the whole picture when details are so important?

I use my wife's "binoculars" approach and look at

the problem at hand using two sides of imaginary binoculars. By looking through the magnifying side of them I see more details. From the opposite side I see the bigger picture – details are not that visible. By using two sides of my mental binoculars I can group related details together into the bigger tasks and worry about details later.

I know that many of our dreams don't get realized because we do not go for it in the present moment. We always look back remembering and analyzing our past, or fast-forwarding to the future, imagining how it may or may not be happening. Both approaches take us from the present moment where the real life is going on. Most of the time we are not present in the here and now, instead missing a lot of potential to manifest our dreams. The main strategy in achieving any future goal is to make a plan and do something that leads us to that goal every day. By doing small steps today, in the present moment, we are living our life's dreams now. When the future we desire comes along, we are ready to achieve the next step leading to our goal in this future "now".

I decide to look at one major question at a time. First of all, am I ready to climb Mt. Everest?

I believe I am. My climbing experience spans over decades. I am physically fit and technically pretty good. My favorite climbing environment is snow and ice – this is what I will mostly have out there. I do not have enough high altitude experience, but I know that I usually feel well at the high altitude and need much less adjustment time than the other people on my previous teams. I have high hopes in this regard.

Notes After

Some people think that climbing Everest is physically challenging, yet easy in terms of having a "walking" climb. Do not trust this opinion. Do not be fooled by the idea that all you need is to be physically fit and to know how to attach yourself to the fixed ropes with ascenders or how to put crampons on. This climb is nothing like that.

There are a couple of things to consider. As a big physical challenge, the Mt. Everest climb requires maximum efficiency from a climber. This efficiency is mostly related to a good technique and can only come from years of mountaineering experience. Good climbing technique relates to all aspects of climbing at high altitudes: breathing, cramponing, using ropes, ability to adjust and function under difficult weather conditions, good orientation, self-reliance and much more.

If a climber does not have an adequate experience and tries to take the mountain by force, it is very inefficient. In other mountains the reserve of one's strength might compensate the lack of efficiency, but not on Everest.

Well-coordinated athletes will find it relatively easy to learn a couple of techniques associated with cramponing. However, real ease and efficiency comes with time and experience. Novices will find themselves not trusting crampons and overusing some group of muscles very quickly. Such climbers will be constantly catching their pants in the crampons and tripping over them, putting themselves and others in dangerous situations.

There is also a significant amount of mixed climbing where ice and rocks are intermixed. It definitely comes into play during the last two days of the climb when climbers wear oxygen masks and bulky down suits. Yellow Band, Geneva Spur, Hillary Step and its vicinity all require an ability to move efficiently on mixed terrains and use ones crampons on rocks.

The second major issue to think about is what is going to happen if I don't reach the top. I need to have a very clear idea about what my definition of success and failure is and decide how to deal with both, potentially. From what I know from the books, there are two ways to deal with this. The first approach is "all or nothing," which means, "I will be successful only if I get to the top, anything less than that is unacceptable to me and will be a failure." Another approach is a "compromise": "It would be great if I just get to Camp 4. The summit is a bonus."

I know that the "all or nothing" scheme is a dangerous one. This is a thinking process that leads many people to their death in mountains and Mt. Everest specifically. People with such mentality are often unable to monitor their condition correctly and pursue their goals no matter what. I believe that the goal of any climb is not just to get to the top, but also to safely get down. On Everest the task of getting down is even more expanded: you have to get down safely, without putting everyone around you in danger. I do not believe that your teammates will simply leave you out there to die. They will try to rescue you and by doing so they will be exposed to great danger.

The second "compromise" approach might not work for me though. I believe in the law of attraction, so I know that the universe will provide me with what I am asking for. When I set up my goal and focus my attention on my intention, I am facilitating the execution of my goal. If I constantly set my attention to get only to Camp 4, most likely I will get there and climb no further.

I am contemplating my approach to this dilemma. First of all, I believe that I can get to the summit. I have visualized myself on the summit and climbed it many times in my dreams. I clearly see myself succeeding in going over the Hillary step and the summit ridge in my visualization. From now on I will imagine myself there when I've already climbed Everest. I put my attention on the goal of reaching the summit.

Being a climber for many years I like the process of climbing. For me it is the most enjoyable part. Of course, I want to get to the top, but the process is even more important. The idea of "all or nothing" feels very foreign to me. Being there, in the mountains, always puts me "in the moment." It means I am in the highest state of awareness, present to my surroundings and my physical and mental state. Having that habit, I trust myself that when and if the time comes to make a decision about turning back, I will be able to make the decision that is right for me. I have that trust in myself and put the question on the back burner, so I can concentrate on my goals without any fear.

So what happens if I don't get to the top?

The answer is I would enjoy every moment of the expedition. I know that I can make it if the circumstances are good. I am confident that I can control my inner states, respond accordingly to the outer conditions, and make a proper decision when and if the time comes. I am going for it.

November 2008 – Family Circle

T here are four of us around the dinner table in our kitchen: my wife, our son Yan who is now 26 years old, and our 23 year old daughter Olya. I am presenting my case, soliciting their feedback. I need them to help me make the right decision on what company to choose for my Everest expedition.

I am explaining to them the two options that I basically have: a guided or a non-guided expedition. There are two major differences between the two: the price of the trip and assistance of western guides. Guided expedition cost is usually much higher, starting at approximately $45,000 and up. Most of the American companies will charge around $65,000. Non-guided expedition price can be between $30,000 and $45,000. None of these prices include equipment, air tickets to Nepal, or any other logistics that should be taken care of in addition to the expedition itself.

Unless you are a part of a particular team and have very meticulous needs that a group trip cannot satisfy, all commercial group expeditions provide full service: flights to Lukla from Kathmandu, porters and logging on the way to the Everest Base Camp, all food and cooks, Sherpas' support to build all camps and usually one to one Sherpa support on the summit day.

Most of the guided expeditions provide the western guides, usually one guide per three clients. The options to participate in guided expeditions, I explain, will not work for me. First of all, we cannot afford it. Second of all, I feel that I have enough experience and will be pretty comfortable on my own. I know that many people feel more comfortable if they are "under the wing" of a western guide and it would be a major decision making point for them. I am interested in having more freedom and being able to make my own decisions.

You probably have seen this group dynamics on the Discovery Channel's "Everest: Beyond the Limit" when Russell Brice is making his final decision about who will or will not go for the Summit. In actuality such leaders make many additional very important decisions related to numerous other aspects of the climb: acclimatization strategy, climbing and oxygen strategy, and so on. Apparently, it makes a lot of sense when such experienced guides are making all these decisions, but from what I have learned during my investigation of this matter, in some cases people rely so much on the guide's supervision that they do not even know how much oxygen they've used, how many bottles they had, etc. This over-reliance makes clients depend on their guides too much and such dependency is an unsafe practice in the high altitude.

In non-guided trips the expedition leader and Sherpas will give you much advice and provide you with their expertise, which will help you, make your own decision. If I take this approach I will be very aware of all the details and possibilities. The leader of the expedition will still have the power to stop me from climbing, but this power will not be exercised unless it is necessary.

Non-guided expeditions are mostly provided by local Nepalese companies or some companies owned by westerners who live in Nepal. If I choose the "full service" non-guided trip, I will get the same infrastructure as I would in a guided expedition in terms of camps, food, cooks and Sherpas etc. Yet, I will not be guided. Rather I will be led by an experienced leader, working with a team of experienced Sherpas. With "full service" I will have my own tent in Base Camp where I will hold all my gear and one to one Sherpa support on the summit day.

I spent tons of time reading multiple websites and blogs before presenting my case. I know that I do not want to participate in guided expedition. I cannot justify paying the high price when I feel comfortable making my own decisions. What I really do not want is to climb alone, or to have a random climbing partner on my ascent. For that reason I am thinking of upgrading my package with an option of a personal Sherpa.

After considering all the options, I am looking into hiring one of two companies. One of them is Asian Trekking, a Nepalese company that was highly recommended by Paul Adler, the Australian climber who was the most valuable resource of information for me, and for whose support I am deeply grateful. Another company sounds similar. It is led by a westerner who led many such expeditions but does not include western guides.

We are bouncing ideas back and forth – my family does not want me to make decisions based on the price. They do not want me even to consider that aspect and ask me to only concentrate on the safety issues. I have to trust my intuition and I know that my safety very much depends on me being present all the time, monitoring my conditions and making right decisions based on my judgment, not someone else's.

What do we know about Asian Trekking?

Not much. Their website does not provide a lot of information (this was true in the beginning of 2009 and it is much different now), but I am digging deep into their success records and see that many professional climbers used them as a support team for their expeditions. I Google people who summited in their teams in previous years, finding their websites, emails, and communicating with them. All responses are very positive. The other company that I also feel good about is much smaller, and it is difficult to find real people to talk to about their experience with the company. They are also a little more expensive. I have to admit that by this time "a little" means we are looking at the range of $5,000. This is by no means a small amount for us, but it is not that much in comparison to the overall cost of the trip.

We take a vote and Asian Trekking it is!

Notes After

After coming back from the climb I can happily say that the decision that we made was the correct one. In my expedition with the Asian Trekking company, in addition to the summit day Sherpa support, every climber was also paired up with a climbing Sherpa on all climbing days. This was really great; I believe in that sense, we had even more support than the guided expedition would be providing.

I saw many guided teams and observed the following: all the climbers in these expeditions move together which means that they move as fast as their slowest climber. To me, this is one of the major disadvantages of guided expedition. There are places on the route, such as Khumbu Icefall, that require moving fast for the most safety leverage.

Further, I was extremely pleased with Dawa Steven Sherpa, our expedition leader, and the whole team that helped us to get to the top. Our lead climber was Apa Sherpa – the world record keeper of most Everest Summits. On May 21, 2009 he reached the summit for 19th time. Many climbers on my team came that year for the second or third attempt to climb Mt. Everest and many of them switched to Asian Trekking from the other companies.

I had a personal Sherpa who was assigned to me and followed me all the time while I was climbing. On the summit day I was accompanied by two Sherpas. It might have given me a feeling of more safety, but one should not rely on that option. In my case, my personal Sherpa Thukten and I moved much faster than my second "team" Sherpa who got to the summit one hour later. I actually did not see him until we got back to the South Col. How ironic!

February 2009 – Screams From the Basement

My wife is rushing down into the basement: "What is going on? Are you okay?"

Yes, I am still okay, just cannot hold the screams that coming out of my body, especially from my burning legs. I am in my third month of training with the P90X program. My sister gave it to me as a gift and I found it very useful not just as my training but also as a simulation of struggle – experience that I definitely need to be trained for.

My physical training is an ongoing effort. I am usually in the gym at least five days a week. My main routine is always to climb the Stair Master escalator wearing a back pack filled with 50 lbs. of training weights and wearing heavy Nikken shoes that add 2.5 lb. to each of my legs. I usually go for an hour at a time. Running is also a part of the weekly routine when I would run for an hour to hour and a half. That was all before the Everest training.

I thought I had to improve my training and add some more science to it. In my favorite climbing book *Extreme Alpinism* by Mark Twight, there is a whole chapter related to physical training. However, his routines are more relevant to a very active climber who spends most of his/her time climbing. I believe they are not so effective for someone like myself, as most of my training was conducted in the gym. At the same time his book gave me a great start in understanding the theory behind optimized training. To follow his advice I would need to conduct some tests that would allow me to understand my specific physiology. As I was not prepared to invest a lot of time and money in the lab tests, I decided to develop my own program based on my understanding.

First, I had to establish a goal for my training: I had to improve my anaerobic threshold. I have read scientific explanations on the topic and understand the following: every one of us has a maximum heart rate – the rate that your heart will not go over regardless of the exercise intensity.

Usually people can maintain their maximum heart rate for only short period of time and then the body goes into an anaerobic state. Anaerobic state is used by sprinters. As a climber, I needed to learn to maintain my so-called aerobic state – the state that I can withstand for hours. The heart rate between aerobic and anaerobic state is called anaerobic threshold and I would need to find out what it is for me.

There are multiple formulas to determine ones maximum heart rate. They are usually connected to the person's age and it varies a lot from person to person even of the same age. In my opinion, these formulas are good for the average person, but cannot be relied upon by serious athletes.

I have used a very simple method to determine my maximum heart rate. I conducted a test on the treadmill wearing the heart rate monitor. I warmed up for 10 min and then started gradually increasing the speed of the machine. Every time I moved to the next speed, my heart rate went up until I had reached 174 beats per minute. Even though I kept increasing the speed after I reached this number, my heart rate did not go up. It was my maximum heart rate. It was a pretty fast run for me and I could not sustain it for more than a couple of minutes.

In order to determine my anaerobic threshold, I used my Stair Master to simulate my climb. It took me a couple of days to understand that at the rate of 152 – 155 bits per minute I could stay on the Stair Master for a long time. As soon as I would increase the speed and go over that limit, I could not continue walking for more than 3 to 5 minutes. My anaerobic threshold was 152. According to the science, my reserve was the difference between the maximum heart rate and anaerobic threshold that for me was 174-152 = 22 bits per minute.

It was interesting that during my run on the treadmill I could maintain a higher heart rate for longer periods of time than when I was just walking around carrying the backpack. It leads me to believe that some strain on the body related to the anaerobic threshold is connected to the weight of my backpack because more muscles are involved in supporting the weight and it requires more oxygen.

Even though I was a bit paranoid, I was not planning to carry my heart rate monitor with me on the mountain to watch it every minute. I had to learn to feel when I was about to reach my anaerobic threshold. As I mentioned before, one can only withstand that high level of intensity for a very short period of time and then the body needs a break to recover. If one stays at this level for a long time, the recovery time increases exponentially and sometimes it needs days to come back to the normal state.

For my Everest training I also added 5 lb. ankle

weights to simulate my heavy boots and crampons that, with my backpack weight, add up to a total of 65 lbs. Every week I would do also at least two interval trainings on the Stair Master machine with my backpack, shifting between speed numbers 3 and 6 for at least five 3-minutes intervals.

Right now I am doing P90x. This means that today I already went through my Stair Master routine during my lunch hour and now, at evening, I am panting and puffing and screaming going through the P90X torture in my basement. I do not execute all 12 DVDs that come with the program, but play only five of them.

Today I am doing my leg routine. I am doing these routines to improve my endurance, leg strength and upper body strength without gaining any muscle weight. The theory here, again, is to have weights light enough, so I can do it for a longer time. The screams come from the repetition numbers between 12 and 15, not 7 or 8 as it would be if I needed to gain muscle weight. I am also doing P90X yoga that I found to be one of the hardest and most important routines for me.

What is very beneficial to me in all P90x routines is that they all have aerobic exercises as well as muscle training. I am not wearing my heart rate monitor, but I am pretty sure that I come close to my threshold more than once.

My weekly training schedule looks like this:

5 days a week at lunch time – Stair Master intervals routines

4 to 5 evening sessions per week – alternating P90 X routines

Saturdays – running for 1.5 hours

Sunday – rest

It does not seem like a lot, does it?

Notes After

At the beginning of the pre-climb training, my reserve (the difference between the maximum heart rate and my anaerobic threshold) was good, but I managed to reduce it. By the time I went to the expedition I had my anaerobic threshold at 160 bpm instead of 152 bpm. I had a chance to test it when I actually crossed my threshold during the climb. Interestingly enough it was not during my ascend, but when I was descending from Camp 3.

Being new to such extreme altitudes, I decided that I could go down faster, especially because I felt very confident with my ice and rope techniques. I started running down the Lhotse Face, bypassing many climbers on the way down, only to find myself out of breath very soon. I stopped for a short while, but was drawn to continue running down by the pride of being so fast. After three of four ropes I found myself almost losing consciousness. At that time I stopped for a longer period of time, but could not recover fully. I was completely out of strength, weak in my knees, and gasping for air. When I finally reached the bottom of the Lhotse Face, I sat there for at least 30 minutes, trying to regain my strength. I could hardly walk and it took a lot of will power to get down to Camp 2. This was a perfect example of crossing my anaerobic threshold. I am sure that my heart rate went through the roof there.

March 2009 – Packing

*T*he time has come! There is only one week left before my flight to Nepal. Our basement is my current front line where all supplies, equipment and clothes are laying everywhere in small and big piles. My preparation of the expedition equipment started a long time ago, but there is no end to this process. I am using my laptop with an Excel file, including 309 lines ranging from something as big as a down suit, to small items such as needles and threads for repairs. I am proud of my spread sheets – they have all of the information about every single item I might possibly need. The spreadsheet lists: the category it belongs to, the climbing sack that it will be put on, the travel duffle bag it will be carried in, and the camp at which it will be used. It allows me to sort my items in any way I want. For instance, I can see what is located in each duffle bag in case it is lost during my travel or check what I planned to use in Camp 4. Because some items will be used all the time, I need to manage their migration from camp to camp, so it is also prepared for close monitoring in my file.

Because of the "high" reliability of our airlines and limitation on the weight that I can bring with me in my two pieces of checked luggage, I am planning to carry all my irreplaceable summit gear with me or directly on me.

This expedition is very different than anything I've encountered before. A lot of equipment and clothes are duplicated. The reason is that some of my stuff will stay permanently at Base Camp and some will be staged in Camp 2. For instance, I have two sleeping bags: one for Base Camp and another for Camp 2 and up, which is a common tactic. I have not decided yet which one goes where. My old one that I used in Alaska and Alps is rated 0°F. It is comfortable and, in addition to our bodies, can accommodate all the items that we usually put inside during the night: two water bottles, socks for the next day, cameras, boots or just inner boots, gloves etc. It is always amazing how much "stuff" goes in when the outside temperature drops below freezing. In upper camps I am planning to sleep in my down suit, so I think that 0°F bag will be good enough. My second bag is rated -20°F. It is a little heavier and a little narrower, so I most likely will use it in Base Camp, where I do not need to hide so much stuff inside.

I also have two pair of climbing boots. My goal is to be ready for the summit day and achieve it while spending the least amount of energy possible. Climbing with lighter boots between Base Camp and Camp 2 will reduce my muscle fatigue dramatically. I will be using La Sportiva Nepal Extreme boots between Base Camp and Camp 2 that weigh only 2.5 lbs. each versus my La Sportiva Olympus Mons High altitude boots that are one pound heavier. I used my La Sportiva High Altitude boots climbing Grant Teton in winter just to test them before my Mt. Denali climb in 2007.

Notes After

There was another benefit of using lighter boots: I could move faster which affected my safety. I missed the tragic avalanche of May 5th that killed Lhakpa Sherpa only by 25 min. Who knows what would be my descend time if I would be wearing heavier boots.

By the time I was ready for the summit, my summit boots were in Camp 2, and for the first two days of the summit push I did not use them at all. This allowed me to keep them really dry. If I would start my ascend in my summit boots from the Base Camp, I would be wearing them for at least four days in a row before the summit day.

I was also using La Sportiva light hiking boots for hiking to the Base Camp and wearing them at Base Camp. It was the right decision to bring them with. On the way to the Base Camp the weather was perfect, but on the way down we encountered a heavy snowfall and two days of rain. It would be very uncomfortable to wear the gym shoes instead of hiking boots as some of our team members did. In addition, after almost twenty days of hiking to and from the Everest Base Camp and walking many days around the Base Camp for acclimatization and exercise, my boots were completely worn out. I could not imagine that any gym shoes could withstand such heavy abuse.

I am holding my new ice axe with tenderness and love. I spent many hours choosing the right one for this expedition and not just because it is the most important climbing gear on Everest. Most of the route will be supplied with the static rope (the rope that is anchored to the ice or rocks, so the climbers can be clipped to it for protection). As you climb using your sliding carabiner or ascender that connects you to the rope, the ice axe is carried in your back pack or holstered in your harness. The ice axe on Mt. Everest becomes very useful in case of some difficult or extraordinary circumstances such as self-rescue or looking for a route in bad weather.

I also know that the ice axe will be the main article on display in pictures from the summit. So, I sold my old ice axe and replaced it with this new one, yellow, which is my favorite color. I think it will look nice with my red down suit. I also made myself a very fancy extendable ice axe leash that I plan to hook to my harness. When I need to extend my hand, it easily extends and contracts back when I do not need it, making it as short as possible, so I do not trip on it. In that case I would not need to switch the leash from hand to hand as ice axe technique requires switching sides while zigzagging.

I am looking at my new down suit. It looks huge, lying on the basement floor filled with air like all down things are. I often try to amaze my friends and relatives who come over to check on my preparations by wearing it with my enormously large high altitude climbing boots. In all this the outfit I look like an astronaut in a space suit and impress everyone, much to my satisfaction.

Most Everest climbers usually use either a full body down suit such as mine or a separate parka and pants. The down suit is considered to be much warmer. Even though I chose to wear it, I am still not sure that it was the right decision. Of course, like with my other climbing gear, I had to make some customizations to it. Even though I was planning to take a spare pair of mittens for the summit day in case I lose my main mittens, I still decided to protect them and make my life more convenient. All climbing mittens come with wrist loops, but I do not like them as their straps are usually too long. When you take off a mitten, it hangs down too low and has a tendency of getting some snow inside.

I made some loops from the elastic cord and sewed them to the internal part of the down suit sleeves. I would use tiny carabiners to connect these straps with the mittens hand loops. This way, if I take my mitten off and accidentally drop it, it would be drawn up by the elastic cord. This design came to me from remembering the time when I was a child and my mom tied my mittens together with a long elastic strap that went from one sleeve's edge to another under my coat, making its way through across my shoulders. I actually tried that old Russian design first, but found my new design to be much better.

Notes After

I wore my down suit just a handful of times. First, it was at Camp 2 at night just to try it on. It was not that cold, but I was checking how it would work out together with my new sleeping bag. At that time I discovered that my bag was too tight for such a combination.

The second night I used it at Camp 3. Again, the

night was not too cold (or at least I was not cold) and I thought that I would be better off in two separate pieces because I did not need that much warmth on my legs.

On my summit day I was warm and my down suit zipper was a little open. On the way down it was so warm that I had to pull down the top part of my down suit and tie it around my waist (which was very inconvenient). At this point I would've been much happier with the two separate pieces and to be able to take the parka off. I took the down suit completely off in Camp 4 and did not use it on my way down to Camp 2 at all.

A separate parka would have also given me another option of using it as a blanket, covering my sleeping bag. In that case I would add significant warmth without compromising my space inside the sleeping bag. It is almost impossible to cover yourself with the full body down suit as it cannot be opened completely and constantly slides from the bag.

The next impressive pile on my basement floor is all my electronic equipment. I had three goals in mind choosing my electronics. First – and most importantly – was to be able to communicate with my family. My second goal was to support my safety on the route. I wanted to be able to communicate with Base Camp at any time. The third goal was to entertain myself. The last goal should not be taken too lightly as I know that the mental state during a long expedition like this one is one of the major elements of success. Entertainment or lack of it can be the difference between willingness to climb to the top or deciding to abort and go home.

I will be using a Thuraya satellite phone for phone calls, as well as a modem for sending emails. I have two SIM cards. The first one to use at Base Camp, Camp 2, and Camp 3 as the minutes on it are much cheaper. I will use the second, more expensive card, on the summit. The Everest summit is on the border with China, and China is not on the list of countries where the first SIM card can be used.

I am taking a small laptop that I will be using to write my blog. The plan is to send my posts via emails to my son who will publish them.

I have two mp3 players with plenty of audio books and movies stored on them. One of them is the old tiny player that can last for 20 hours on a single AAA battery. I treasure it because it is difficult to find something like that these days. It will go to the upper camps with me where I will not have access to power for recharging. The second one has a small screen and I am planning to finish a couple of seasons of *Prison Break* and watch some movies.

I also have two digital photo cameras. One is the main camera and another one is a backup for summit day. The plan is to carry one of them on me and give the second one to my Sherpa. Again, my back up camera was chosen because it works on AA batteries that can be replaced if the cold kills the first set of batteries.

I have a small but expensive solar recharge system to recharge my players and the phone at upper camps. Asian Trekking will provide larger solar power batteries to recharge my computer and other equipment at Base Camp.

My medical stuff is next. I know that staying healthy during this expedition will be a challenge which is another factor that can make a difference between an expensive attempt and a priceless success. At high altitudes, especially on Everest, anything that goes wrong with your health tends to progress very fast. I have all kind of pills with me for all sorts of common problems such as cold or upset stomach as well as for illnesses specifically related to the altitude sicknesses such as pulmonary and cerebral edema. In order to save room and make it more convenient to use, I packed the groups of pills together in small containers. Some will accompany me on the trek, some will stay at Base Camp, and some will be carried with me during my acclimatization climbs and to the summit. Each container has a list of pills that are inside with the description of their usage, color and shape, so I can differentiate between them. I already packed a couple of Dexamethasone and Nifedipine pills in my down suit pocket that will be respectively used in case of emergency against cerebral or pulmonary edema. Together with some sanitary supplies, this bag alone is almost 5 lbs.

I am also carrying an extensive repair kit. I planned it carefully, but now, looking at its size, I see that I can open small repair shop at Base Camp and compensate for the money invested into the expedition.

There are many items that I have modified or made specifically for this expedition. As I mentioned, my love to modify equipment came from the old days in Russia, where we could not buy any equipment in the stores. My unsettled mind cannot rest even here in America, where we have an abundance of equipment.

During my first skiing trip to Colorado with my family in 1991 I quickly discovered that it was very tiring to take inner boots out of the ski boots every evening to dry them. After all I had to take care of all four pair of boots. I immediately came up with the idea to use the dryer for drying our boots. The idea was so brilliant and I was so confident in positive results, that I not only took the four pairs of boots that belonged to my family, but also collected boots from many of my friends, promising them an unparalleled result. As one might imagine, the high temperature of the dryer and the long rotation cycle melted the glue, separating many parts of our inner boots from each other. I ended up matching parts together and convincing everyone that all the minor parts that were left over after this project were not needed in the first place.

This small setback in my invention experience did not change my desire to improve things. I have been continuously improving my ski boot drying technique. My next invention was to use lighting in order to dry my boots. What is really needed to dry the boots overnight is to facilitate a convection process inside the boot, concentrating especially in the toe area. This area is not only the most important part to dry, but also the most difficult. Some kind of small fans would work great there, but would make noise. And to have eight fans for four pairs of boots was also unreasonable. I needed a source of warmth that can be small enough to be inserted deep into a boot, but not too hot so that it would burn the inner lining. I clearly envisioned a long wire that can be plugged into the electrical outlet with a garland of 5″ ceramic cylindrical heating elements evenly spread along so that each can be inserted into one boot. The resistance of each element has to be calculated in a way that an element would produce about 90° to 100° F. What could I use that would provide the same result without getting in the way of production of my imaginary garland?

The answer was Christmas lighting. It was perfect. I would arrange all four pairs of boots in a single row, stick multiple little lamps inside of each boot and continue doing so from boot to boot. The only side effect of this invention was a bright light coming from my "drying center" during the night, so sometimes we would cover all these boots with a towel or would arrange the boots in the corner where the light would be less disturbing.

At that time my wife was organizing group ski trips every year. They mostly consisted of our friends and their friends, but sometimes our group would have 20 people, sometimes 50 and once we even had about 70 participants. We, of course, shared our lighting invention with everyone in the group and it was funny to see Christmas lighting in the many condos occupied by our group. Later on I replaced Christmas lighting with a tube lighting that works just as well, but is more durable.

Before the Mt. McKinley climb I decided to make a very light backpack to use for summit day. I looked at some available light backpacks, but none of them matched my requirements. I was inspired to make my own, using a very lightweight advanced fabric, so it would weigh around 1 lb. I spent many weekends constructing and reconstructing it. I wanted it to be useful not only on the summit day, but during the whole expedition so it would not be a dead weight during our multiday approach. I made it convertible into the sleeping bag compression sack. It was pretty difficult to do, but I succeeded, However, I decided against taking it to Mt. Everest because of the large amount of rock climbing sections such as Hillary Step and Geneva Spur where it could be accidentally torn apart by rocks and lose its contents.

From my reading and understanding of Everest climbing I knew that an ascender is one of the major pieces of climbing gears that is being used there every day. As I mentioned before, an ascender is a smart device that allows climbers to slide it up the rope, but it will not slide back in case of the fall. Most climbers use the Petzl Ascension ascender. However, its handle is rather small for a big glove and especially for the expedition mitten that I was planning to wear on the summit day. I have been practicing using it at home with my mittens or gloves on. Even though I could use it without taking my mittens off, I knew that it would be much easier to have a larger handle.

My solution was to replace the handle of my ascender completely, making it big enough for my big Outdoor Research mitten to easily slide in. With the help of my friend Efim, we made a new handle much larger than the original one out of a very light aluminum plate. We then cut the existing handle and attached the new one using four screws.

The most time was spent on designing my own warming system for my extremities. Most people utilize a Hotronic warming system that uses some thin heating electrical elements, attached to the insole of the boots with rechargeable batteries to feed them. Even though many climbers reported good results with this device I did not want to rely on it. One of the major disadvantages of these batteries is that they last only six hours and definitely cannot be recharged during the summit climb. To take two sets of these batteries would be very expensive and not practical as I would need to carry them up and down myself. I am not describing the details of my solution in here, because I want to get it patented. For the record, I started working on it in 2007 with my friend Arnold before my Mt. Denali climb. What we've created worked very well; it lasted for 10 hours and was much less expensive. For the Everest climb I redesigned internal parts of the system and my friend simplified the exterior. The system was so simple that I decided not only to use it for my feet, but also for warming up my hands.

Notes After

The system worked perfectly well and my feet and hands were very warm during my entire summit climb. I even managed to use my bare hands to take pictures and sometimes was switching ropes near the anchors with my uncovered hands: I was confident that they would be instantly warmed up as soon as I put my mittens back on.

Part 2 – The Expedition

April 2, 2009 – In Kathmandu

I am in Katmandu. The flight went much easier than I expected. The longest wait was in London, where I spent eleven hours laying on a nice soft bench in the middle of the shopping center in Terminal 3. It was a little challenging not to lose the spot during my toilet breaks, so I would wait for someone to sit near me and ask them to watch my luggage.

I got into the O'Hare International airport completely prepared to scale Everest. I was wearing my climbing soft shell pants, my Patagonia soft shell jacket and my La Sportiva Eva climbing boots. My first big carry-on backpack was skillfully filled with my huge high altitude boots, summit down suit, expedition mittens and other summit clothes. The second small carry-on backpack had all electronics, computer, and my satellite phone. I was prepared to survive catastrophic (but not unusual) situations if my luggage would be lost. I also was prepared to survive emergency landing on North Pole. As soon as I went through security in order not to get a heatstroke I had to go to the restroom and change back to the normal clothes that I was also carrying. All the gear that I was wearing just a moment ago went into a huge plastic bag that was strategically positioned in one of the backpack pockets. What one will not do to survive!

The flight to Bahrain on Gulf Air was not that significant. It was very nice to receive a large menu for dinner in coach. However, my expectations were not met. Two and a half hours after the menu was delivered we were given just what was left in their kitchen. No choices and no questions asked.

On the last leg from Bahrain to Katmandu I was unexpectedly given a business class seat instead of my assigned coach seat. However, the flight was relatively short, just four hours, so I spent the whole time learning how to move my seat in five different directions, switching on and off my new individual TV screen and trying to find an even more comfortable position.

There was another advantage to being in the business class: I was the first one to receive my new Nepalese Visa. It took me just five min and $100. It looked like the Nepalese learned how to take money very efficiently. To my joyful surprise all my luggage arrived safely and I was given the green light to exit the Customs area. Asian Trekking representatives met me at the exit and I was introduced to the craziest driving I have ever experienced.

As I discovered on my first day in Kathmandu, six months was not enough time to pack all that I needed for the Everest expedition. I ended up forgetting my music. I had to log in remotely to my home computer and transfer my music files to my website. Later I downloaded it from there to my laptop that I had with me. At least it gave me something to do.

The streets of the touristy shopping district of Kathmandu are narrow and both sides are filled with small stores. Every third store sells climbing and trekking equipment. All famous brands are present – The North Face, Mountain Hardwear, etc. All are made in Katmandu and all are fake. I could not contain myself and bought a nice balaclava, two duffle bags for doubling mine in case of rain or rough carrying on yaks. I also bought a spare pair of down mittens – all for a fraction of the price we pay in the U.S.

The streets are full of people, bikes, and cars. It is now clear why people have to stay in Kathmandu for some time before they go to Everest. I think it's a test. If you survive the traffic on the streets of this city without getting killed or having a heart attack, you are ready to go.

Ready to climb

April 7 – To Lukla

Our team is ready to fly to Lukla. Asian Trekking cars pick us up from the hotel and drive us to the airport. It is 6:30 a.m.

It is extremely crazy there. Each of us has between two to three huge duffle bags full of equipment and other stuff. These bags are divided into two piles: one goes with us on the trek, another goes straight to Base Camp. Many expeditions have been trying to fly out to Lukla for a few days now. The weather in Lukla is not good and after six – seven hours of waiting a lot of people are sent back to the hotels and have to start over the next day.

The system here is particularly unique. Because we are scheduled to fly today, we are put in front of the line in comparison to people whose flight was canceled yesterday. If our flight is canceled today, we would need to go to the end of the line for tomorrow. So we hope today is our lucky day.

It is difficult even to get to the terminal. All the bags that are going into the terminal are scanned right at the entrance to the terminal, creating a huge line. Our Sherpas know what to do as well as the Sherpas from other expeditions. It is a competition of knowledgeable people trying to get in fast. We are all afraid to lose our bags in this nightmare because we are separated from our luggage. Inside of the terminal we see the piles of bags. They are everywhere and some of them are 3 to 4 meters high. In addition to our bags, there are tons of team equipment that Asian Trekking needs to fly to

Lukla. They chartered the biggest possible helicopter for that. As the day goes on there are multiple delays. At the end of the day we have to go back to the hotel, back to the Kathmandu streets, breathing dusty air, hoping for tomorrow.

Today is our second day at the airport. It feels exactly like the first one – delays, lots of people, bags, but today we are at the end of the line. Some teams do not have patience and leave the airport. Apa and Pertemba Sherpas are working their connections, so our team is still there, waiting and hoping. At 4:00 p.m. the weather window opens up and we are on the plane. We are in!!! Nothing can stop us now.

45 minutes later we are landing in a very unusual manner. The landing strip in Lukla goes up at a 10 to 15 degree angle, so we land uphill. The climb has already started!

Our team at Lukla Airport

April 10 – Namche Bazaar

I am so excited! Not only because I am on the trek to the most famous Base Camp in the world and will see the tremendous Namche Bazaar, but also because I will see my wife who is coming down the trek from that same Base Camp. She had left Chicago a week before me, leading her client on a spiritual journey. She reached the Everest Base Camp and climbed Kala Patar at 5500m. I am amazed by this achievement and so proud of her. Our delays at the airport were designed by the universe to give us the opportunity to meet on the trek in such a remarkable place. Had we left on time from Kathmandu, we would have missed each other on the trek.

This morning the trek ran along the river, crossing multiple bridges. After lunch we reached Jorsale, the last village before Namche Bazaar. Here the trek goes up pretty steep and gains 800 m (2600ft) of altitude reaching 3400m at Namche. It usually takes 2.5 – 3 hours to get up to Namche. That is 2.5 hours for normal people, not some crazy Germans like my friend Henry, who decided to sprint the distance. Being competitive and trying to see my wife as soon as possible, I am determined to keep up with him. At the end I lost him, reaching Namche in 1 hour 30 minutes. It felt great even though I was a little tired.

Namche is an amazing place. It sits on narrow cirques, forming a semicircular hollow with steep walls formed by glacial erosion on mountains. All the buildings are built out of light stone that is manually cut somewhere nearby.

As soon as we reached the lodge, it started raining and then snowing really hard. I was sitting in the common area of our hotel constantly monitoring the entry door, waiting for Sveta. And there she was, in a poncho and a funny hat, smiling and happy. We embraced and it felt so good. We could not stop talking, sharing the latest news and stories.

Our lucky reunion at Namche Bazaar

There was a famous apple pie place in Namche, where they made pastries, so we went for it. We were drifting through the narrow streets of Namche, talking, stopping by the small stores, buying some souvenirs. It was a very special moment for me and the last touch of home before Everest.

April 16 – On the road to Base Camp

T onight is the last night we spend in beds. Tomorrow we will sleep in our tents in Base Camp. In order to spend my time wisely, I am writing about my trekking experience for the next generation of trekkers and climbers.

Trekking to Base Camp took us 12 days. It was two days more than most climbers usually spend as we took a detour to visit Apa Sherpa's home. This trekking time is a very important acclimatization component and we did not want to speed it up and get to Base Camp faster. Our bodies needed this time, and we would not regret it. We took it slowly and enjoyed the scenery.

It was really a huge relief for me to get out of the craziness of Kathmandu after two days of waiting at the airport. I knew that the trek would be the first test of my mental readiness, which includes an ability to take reality as is, without rushing it.

In Kathmandu everyone separated their luggage into two parts. One went directly to Base Camp, and we did not see it for the duration of the trek. I was not sure if our bags would travel on yaks or porters, so I bought extra duffle bags to protect mine. Yaks are not as careful with loads as porters are. They often rub your bags against rocks on the trail which can tear them apart. Some bags traveled with us, but were carried by porters and would be delivered to the next logging by the end of the day. Porters that carry our bags in enormous piles are still faster than us trekking slowly with almost no luggage. Sometimes we would show our macho egos and come to the lodging faster than porters only to discover that there is nothing to change into.

Most people did not carry much in their day pack. I think I was a little different. Being very cautious not to get sick, I was carrying the following items in my day pack at all times:

- Extra base layer
- Patagonia Soft Shell; Patagonia Puff Jacket – two layers that should keep me warm during the trek, even in bad conditions
- Thin warm hat; thin gloves
- Rain gear

The rest of the stuff was standard:

- Sunglasses, sun hat, sun block
- MP3 player
- Medical set with antibiotic against food poisoning and Imodium (because you never know when it can start);
- Foot treatment against blisters
- Toiletries: toilet paper, sanitizer, etc.
- Camera
- Buff or surgical (painter's) mask against dust. Most Sherpas use different kinds of buffs. I took a lot of surgical masks but often could not use them. It was very difficult for me to breathe through them.

Being aware of possible dehydration, I was drinking plenty of water. I usually started my day with two liters of water and carried two additional liters with me. From what I have seen, it is more than most people would carry. I have never regretted it as my backpack was very light and such small investments always pay off for me.

There were multiple small stores along the track, where we could buy bottled water, some snacks and candy bars, so that we could rely solely on those if we wanted to. Our day treks were not so long and time between breakfast and lunch, or lunch and dinner was no more than four hours. I could buy bottled water on my way, but the higher we went, the fewer stores we saw. Some stretches, especially long ascents on the trail such as the one leading to Namche Bazaar, did not have any stores and this was when I needed water the most. (Ascent to Namche can take from 1.5 to 2.5 hours depending on your condition).

During lunch time I would drink some tea and refill my water bottles. I tried to consume at least 4-5 liters of water a day. In addition, I preferred my own snacks that I brought with me from back home. I had mostly Isagenix bars and Isagenix Want More Energy drinks that kept me going. I would take just a couple of bars for a day and leave the rest of my snack supply in my trekking duffel.

Like most teams, we stayed in tea houses: small hotels that were scattered along the trek and mostly concentrated in small villages. These houses do not have a heating system, so it feels pretty cold at night, especially at higher altitude. Rooms can usually accommodate two or three people with beds that even have pillows and blankets. However, we used our own sleeping bags, which were carried in the trekking duffle. It was much more comfortable and sanitary.

Most of the hotels had restrooms inside. Some, however, still had outhouses. Having a pee bottle was very helpful, so I did not have to wonder around in the dark in search of the toilets. Actually, I would not need to wonder in the darkness because I always had my head lamp with me.

April 17 – Everest Base Camp, 5300m

I am at my new home now. Everest Base Camp is going to be my home for the next five weeks! I am trying to get used to the surroundings and this annoying noise produced by the air going in and out when I talk. Soon I understand that getting used to THIS is never going to happen— one cannot get used to this immense beauty, excitement and lack of oxygen. The lack of oxygen is very real; you cannot run or even make a couple of fast steps without losing your breath.

The Base Camp is an astonishing place. It is completely different than I had imagined it. It is situated on a very uneven glacier with some bumps of ice between 2 and 7 meters high rising everywhere. A large portion of the ice is covered with moraine. Tents from many expeditions, large and small, are scattered everywhere. The whole Base Camp extends about 500 meters, gradually rising with the glacier. Our camp is at the top portion of Base Camp at the so called Crampon Point. This point is an entry to the Icefall and to the route to the top. The famous Khumbu Icefall is huge and can be seen right in front of us. It is much bigger than I thought, especially in relation to the tiny figures moving up and down below.

We all have individual three person's tents with foam mats that cover the floor. This is a real luxury. I put all three of my huge duffle bags inside and still have plenty of room. The most amazing thing is the light that hangs from the tent ceiling. It lights up the tent very well even though all this light comes from solar power.

Each expedition builds multiple community tents that include a dining tent, communications tent, as well as a tent for Sherpas. There are also toilets and shower cabins. Our community tent is very long and tall, which allows us to easily walk inside. There is one long table that is made out of small ones in the middle of the dining tent that allows all of us to sit around it using the folded chairs on both sides. The floor is covered with carpet, which is a strange, but very nice feature in this environment. There are always thermoses filled with hot tea and milk tea on the tables. There is a gas heater in the corner and when it works (only after 6:00 p.m.) it is very warm inside the tent.

Our team in the dining tent

We are extremely cautious about hygiene. There is a bucket of hot water outside of the dining tent, so we can wash our hands before eating. Yet before dinner is served, we are given hot moist towels to wipe our hands – who can refuse the luxury?

It's noon now, and the sun is shining. I use my new battery powered trimmer to trim my beard, which has grown a lot since I left home. My oxygen saturation this morning was 78 out of 100 and pulse was 67 which is very good as far as I am concerned. No headaches so far. It has been 19 days since I left home, and we are only at Base Camp. All my previous expeditions would be over by this time. I can feel that this is a very different one

Base Camp wonders

April 22 – Camp 1, 6100m

W hoosh!!!!! I wake up with a huge, deep, spasmodic inhale, as if I have just come back from under water, escaping drowning in the last millisecond of my life.

What was that? What just happened? My heart is jumping out my throat. Am I alive?

Yes you are. But barely. You just stopped breathing. That is all.

What do you mean "stopped breathing"?

Don't you remember people told you about chain stroke breathing? They also call it periodic breathing.

Oh, this is what it is? Is this how you die here?

Don't be so dramatic. This is nothing. It is normal. You are still only at 6100m. Go to sleep and forget about it.

No, I am not going to sleep! I will stay awake. I do not want for this to happen again.

Calm down…Calm down… Breathe. You need your power breathing. Breathe in, breathe out, breathe in, breathe out…

Whoosh!!!! Oh, God! It is happening again. Did I just fall asleep again? I should be awake and breathing, not sleeping. Why can't I just be awake? Breathe. In and out, in and out.

Come on! Be a man! This is Everest. Are you going to be such a chicken? They told you it happens to many people. You need your rest. Go to sleep.

Ok, ok! I am going to sleep… Whoosh!!!! Oh, God! When will it stop?

April 24 – New Record

I am back from my first rotation: Base Camp – Camp 1 – Camp2 – Base Camp. And Wow! I already reached my personal altitude record. My previous one was the top of mount McKinley at 6194m and I just stood there for 30 minutes. In this my first acclimatization rotation I have not only reached Camp 1, but also Camp 2, and slept there. The climb is so beautiful that I want to describe every step that I made.

As soon as we left the crampon point, which is only 10 yards from my tent at Base Camp, we started climbing up through the Icefall. For 20-25 minutes you climb up and down large steep ice formations and do not really gaining the altitude. This part was difficult at the dark when we left because it was the beginning of the climb and instead of getting used to the rhythm of going up or down you're switching back and forth.

On the way back, this section was very disappointing because you could already see Base Camp approximately at the same level as you are. It is so close and clear, but still you need to climb up and down the ice formations.

As soon as you pass this part the real climb begins and you are in the famous Khumbu Icefall. The climb through the Icefall is not technically difficult but very dramatic. You climb in a labyrinth of huge seracs that are sometimes the size of large buildings. The static ropes that are anchored to the ice go from the bottom to the top of the Icefall, and everyone is clipped to them at all times. Climbers use two carabiners to clip to the rope in order to bypass the anchor. You need to use one carabiner to clip higher than the anchor and only after that unclip the second carabiner below the anchor to maintain constant belay. On the more inclined and vertical spans most people use an ascender – a device that allows you to slide it up the rope and does not slides back. I have to admit that even on some vertical ladders I felt pretty comfortable and used just a carabiner even though it did not provide good protection from the possible vertical fall.

On the Khumbu Icefall

This year it took about 25 to 30 aluminum ladder crossings to span large crevasses that could not be crossed by any other means. I trained myself at home in my backyard with such crossings and we also had some practice at Base Camp, but the real thing was a lot more

Yury Pritzker

fun. Most climbers use two ladder steps to place a foot to hook the front teeth of their crampons to one step, and their heel on to the other. Most Sherpas are so used to these ladders that they just use one ladder step and place their feet so that the step is at the middle of the foot. It is not a stable position and to maintain balance they just walk fast imitating street walking. Some crossings are so large that it takes two or three ladders placed tightly together to span them. Usually there are two ropes that hang along the two sides of each ladder used as rails. They are also anchored to the ice so they are just lying on the ground. Before crossing you need to pick them up and hold them in your hands to provide the tension that's supposed to help you keep your balance.

Camp 1, 6100m. Pumori in the background

At the top of Icefall the view widens and you can see the famous Western Cwm – the ice and snow valley surrounded by the Everest shoulder on the left, Nuptse on the right and South Face of Lhotse in front – the fourth highest peak on Earth. If you turn around toward the Icefall you can see the beautiful summit of Pumory.

Camp 1 is not really at the top of the Icefall but approximately 15 – 20 min from the top. So, when you think that you just climbed the Icefall and are expecting to see your tents, there is still some distance to cover. There are many crevasses here as well, so you need to follow the path and be clipped to the rope.

The route from Camp 1 to Camp 2 is not difficult or steep, but rather long, much longer than it looks. The Western Cwm can be very hot when there is no wind and the sun is up. It is like a huge ice bowl that reflects sun from everywhere.

Camp 2 is located on the side of the moraine approximately between 6300m and 6400m. This moraine is actually the steepest part between Camp 1 and Camp 2. I did not know where our tents were and when I first saw the tents of Camp 2, I was relieved to know that we were almost there. To my disappointment, the climb from the first tents to our tents at the top of the Camp 2 took me another 40 minutes of real struggle. The weather that day was not cooperating, as we had strong wind and snow. When I eventually found my tent, I was so tired that I dropped down and lay on my back for a good 10 minutes until I got my senses back.

Camp 2 is a smaller copy of Base Camp. It has a large tent for dining, cooks, toilets. However it is a much colder place and can be very unpleasant if the weather is bad. Here, a lot of people wear their down suits at night. From here the Lhotse face is so close that it seems like you can touch it , but we all know that this is just an illusion.

The next day I woke up at Camp 2 feeling a little dizzy. I did not have any appetite and my head was spinning. I could not understand what was happening and decided that I needed a little more action to start breathing harder. I decided to go up a little higher, moving toward the Lhotse face where the fixed ropes start near the bergschrund (the area of big crevasses that separates the steep and stable part of the glacier from the flat moving part). I felt a little better, but when I came back to Camp 2 the dizziness returned. "Well, no more playing with the altitude," I said to myself, and started descending to Camp 1 where I felt much better. I spent another night there before enjoying the "thick" air of Base Camp.

April 29 – Nesting

*T*oday I decided to reorganize and clean my "one bedroom apartment". I "vacuumed" the floor from the down that floats everywhere using a napkin and organized my furniture in the most optimal manner. As you might imagine, my apartment looks like any good apartment: it has a front and a back door. Both doors have vestibules, and I do use them. My back door vestibule contains one duffle bag where I keep some food that I brought with me. Whatever was tasty at home does not go down so easily now, so this food sits there mostly for intrusion prevention, guarding my back door. The front vestibule has another bag that contains useless stuff that I do not need, just like any typical house.

From the furniture perspective, I have only two other pieces inside: one small nylon bag where I keep only clean clothes (less than 10 days of use) and one big bag that has some useful, but not frequently used stuff. I arranged my shoe shelf at the front door on the right and my electronics in the left deep corner. After all this was done I stopped, looked at it, and decided it was good enough.

My entertainment so far has been watching *Prison Break*. I already finished two seasons containing about 40 episodes and find it very interesting. I am watching them when I go to bed at night for 1.5 or 2 hours or until the hand holding the player gets frozen. My wife's player, that I borrowed for this purpose is working magically, and sometimes I forget where I am.

Sometimes I find myself thinking very hard of nothing for a long time. I think that they call it "being in the moment". Some examples of such thinking are below:

"It is getting pretty warm here at Base Camp during the day and the glacier we are sitting on is melting. The tent ice platforms are getting higher and higher in relation to the uneven, but evenly melting surface of the glacier. Some edges of the tent start hanging over these small cliffs and puddles of water are forming in between tents. During the night, when it's quiet, I can hear some loud pops that come from the glacier – summer is coming."

"Over time the desire to take a shower every day diminishes. Two showers a week is an overwhelming task now."

"I think I lost some weight but it is not a scientific fact yet."

"I am drinking between 4 to 6 liters of liquid a day, yet I am not sure that this is enough. I assume that I produce the same or almost the same amount of liquid myself, but this is not a scientific fact yet either."

"Sometimes during the day or night we can hear ice avalanches setting off around the camp. We only go outside of our tents to watch the big ones – small ones are not that interesting. We can differentiate them by the strength of the sound they produce. We've gotten used to them by now."

"When the sun goes down in the evening, it gets pretty cold here and we gather around our small gas furnace."

"Why do people live in big houses and surround

themselves with so much stuff? The tent with two vestibules is all I need... Maybe I would add another portion to the tent, so I can have a bedroom there and storage here. I would also get a thicker mattress in the bedroom area of my tent and maybe a small flashlight for night reading. By the way, it would be really nice to have a holder for my player so I do not need to hold it with my hands as they get frozen. A little heater would solve the freezing problem, also a water heater, so I do not need to go to the group tent to get hot water. Maybe a small kitchen addition? Good idea. It will require some more investment in stuff... Oh, God!! I am really on a roll here."

My tent at Base Camp

May 1 – Happy May Day

*T*oday I am celebrating May 1 – International Workers' Day and my first month since I left home. I believe it is my longest absence from home in my life. It is time to sit, relax and think about what was achieved over this last month:

1. I am here, in one of the most astounding places on Earth.

2. I do not have the Khumbu cough.

3. I did not get diarrhea on the way up here.

4. I believe I can still count up to 10 even though people say that at altitude brain cells die like crazy.

5. I have already reached 6600m, which is a personal best, and on the way I did not lose any food except the regular way.

6. I have the honor of being in the company of some very famous climbers, who are frequently subjects of articles and photos. I am learning so much from them.

7. I am in the middle of unfolding my Himalayas dream and playing an active part in it.

8. My loved ones and friends are in good health and are supporting me.

9. I am waking up every day to the most beautiful views that anyone can imagine through the open door of my tent!

Today I woke up under a perfect blue sky and saw Base Camp being covered with an inch of fresh snow. As usual, our Sherpas woke us up with a cup of hot tea at 7:45 a.m. or so. Some of our team members recommend we carry out this practice when we come back home. I am writing this down, so that there is no surprise at home when I will not wake up without my morning tea.

Because of the first day of the month and the holiday, I decided to take a shower according to our old Russian tradition: a shower is a holiday and of course any holiday requires a shower. This is a multi-step process and should not be taken lightly.

You need to manage your timing perfectly. First, wait for the middle of the day when the sun is the strongest, but don't overdo it because most afternoons are cloudy. You also have to prepare everything in advance because you would not be able to get back to your tent if you forget something. Actually, you could, but it would be quite unpleasant, running around naked when everyone else is wearing down coats.

The shower itself, just like the toilet, is in a small tent that is built on top of the ice, covered with relatively flat stones. The door has a zipper, so you can have some privacy. You can get warm water from the kitchen and put it in the hand pump that holds about a gallon of water by my estimation. So, you are going in, carrying all your stuff and the pump filled with water.

Then your actions have to be fast and precise. You undress and start pumping to send some pressure to the water tank. This step is actually good, as you are doing something that makes you feel warmer. After this step is done, you need to lean the pump against the tent wall, making sure that it is not going to fall on your feet. Next, you use the hand shower head to release some water. You repeat these steps a couple of times as the pump loses pressure fast. After the shower, I just turn my old clothes inside out before putting them back on (just kidding).

My next step today is to celebrate May 1 as a worker's day by doing some real work. I am going out to collect some Everest garbage near Base Camp. For the second year in a row our Eco Everest Expedition pays cash for garbage that people collect on Everest. We even gave this mission a funny name – Cash-for-Trash. This year the program started slowly, but after one of our team members, Nic, brought 35 kg of garbage and got paid on the spot, the whole idea exploded. Sherpas from all teams stopped climbing and started collecting garbage. We have collected six tons of garbage and it was a record for any such efforts. This garbage has to be carried on porters' backs to some villages down below where it can be put to rest.

Some Sherpas found large pieces of a crashed Italian helicopter that were very heavy and because of their weight started bringing them good earnings. After some difficult calculations of available money supply and weight of the helicopter – even in parts – our expedition leader Dawa Steven Sherpa decided to exclude the helicopter from the acceptable list of garbage. That was a smart move that put some Sherpas' minds back to climbing.

So, this morning I also decided to go garbage hunting. You just go toward the Icefall on the glacier and after five minutes you are in a beautiful maze of ice formations running from 1 to 10 meters high. Because the sun is up pretty high, and the temperature is around 15C, the glacier is melting and multiple rivers run on the surface to somewhere under the ice.

Ice formations frequently open up into big flat areas where one has to be very careful not to get into the water melted under the ice. It was difficult to find any garbage as everyone did a great job collecting it earlier. After 1.5 hours I was able to collect some old ropes and aluminum cans.

On the way back, I decided to test if the flat places on the glacier would give out, and got one of my feet under the surface where it found some ice water. I was quick to pull it back, so the damage was not that great. I also successfully tested the idea that SmartWool socks keep you warm even when they are wet.

In any case, as you can see, the day went on with me fully engaged in celebration and some experimental work. Walking back, I look forward to changing into my down clothes as it is getting a bit chilly. After dinner I will go to my now relatively clean apartment (tent) where I will watch 67th, 68th and maybe 69th episodes of the *Prison Break*. Just another day at the Everest Base Camp...

May 4 – Camp 3, 7200m

*B*y now I've gotten used to the fact that I am reaching my personal records almost every day. Today I slept in Camp 3 at 7200m and was fine!

The decision to "sleep or not to sleep" at Camp 3 without oxygen is a topic of debates between many climbers. People usually do not like to stay there – on a very narrow shelf where the tents are built with limited movement, and for a lot of people it is the most difficult night to survive. Many climbers on the last rotation before the summit bid go to Camp 3, but do not sleep there. I knew that such tactics definitely would reduce my acclimatization preparation and I would be depending much more on supplemental oxygen than others who slept at Camp 3. I also knew that such dependence reduces my safety margin. If something goes wrong with the oxygen system on summit day my ability to move without supplemental oxygen (presumably down) can save my life. So there was no debate for me personally whether to sleep or not to sleep at Camp 3, especially because it would be a good test of my mental readiness to continue.

It takes me an hour to get from Camp 2 to the beginning of the Lhotse face at the bergschrund. As many others, I leave my ski poles at the bergschrund, clip my ascender to the fixed rope of the Lhotse face, and the real fun begins.

The wall is steep, and it is tough. Finally, I reached the place known to me only from books, where you start breathing 3 to 4 breathes per step – welcome to the

Everest altitude! Every 40 m or so there is another anchor to bypass: clip sliding carabiner to the next rope span, unclip ascender and clip it back to rope higher than the anchor, breath four breaths to recover, take a step, breath four times, another step, get to the next anchor, and repeat everything all over again.

There is one more altitude phenomenon that I discovered here which I was not prepared for – the best measurement of distance at such altitude is not feet or meters, but time. It happens when I start clearly seeing people at Camp 3. At this point, I can not only see them but I can also see what they are doing and it still takes me another hour to get there.

I am glad I am wearing my helmet as chunks of ice from the feet of other climbers in front of me are flying around. I also see some other objects falling down – someone's mittens and even a bottle of water. No one told me that you can be killed on Everest by a bottle of water or I would never have come to such place! ! The last 30 feet before our camp are a special treat as they represent almost a vertical bulge of ice.

Camp 3 is located in the middle of Lhotse Face. The platform for the camp is manually carved out of the snow and ice of the face. Room at the camp is very limited and because of this, teams have their camps on different altitudes from 7100 to 7300 meters. There is almost no room to move in the camp, as most of the shelf room is occupied by tents, and if you need to get to some elimination procedures, you better be wearing your crampons, and be clipped to the rope.

It is impossible to describe my feeling of admiration of the view from such a place. It is just magnificent with the whole Western Cwm lying down below and the summit of Pumori just up front almost at the same altitude. You just have to be there to appreciate it.

We eat some soup and for the rest of the day I am drinking water, listening to my books, and trying to perform my power breathing routines as much as possible. During rest time the breathing naturally slows down, and this is the most dangerous time for people to get sick with altitude sickness. In order to avoid it you need to force much deeper breathing with exhales done through tight lips.

The night goes very well and I do not even have chain stroke breathing (when breathing stops completely), which I had experienced in Camps 1 and Camp 2.

Climbing Lhotse wall to Camp 3

May 5 – The Tragedy

We are having breakfast at Camp 2: Nic and I, and the Austrians – Walter, Bernice, Felix and Tomsky. Because most of the Austrian team is here, Lhakpa Sherpa is serving us breakfast with his admirable smile. We are having a good time, ready to get down after reaching Camp 3. Our acclimatization is over and we are prepared for the summit. Nic and I are packed and leaving. The Austrians are still in the camp getting ready to follow us.

It is hot there, in Western Cwm even at such an early hour. My Sherpa, Thukten, is in front of me. He is moving fast, and I am trying to maintain his pace while watching my steps and breathing. Soon we reach Camp 1. Thukten does not stop, going directly down toward the Icefall with me right behind him.

On the Icefall I cannot maintain his pace any longer and he disappears somewhere between seracs. I stop to get rid of some layers, annoyed with Thukten: "Why is he always leaving me alone?" Okay. I am better now, and climbing down as fast as I can to catch up with him. I see him waiting for me at the flat spot on the Icefall. I finally reach him, sweaty as hell. He looks scared, mumbling some words and I know that he is praying. Now he is talking to me, "Fast, fast! Down, down. Too hot!" He is looking at the West shoulder of Everest; its hanging glacier is a cause of constant avalanching.

Now I am as nervous and scared as he is. We are running down again. He is far ahead of me again, so I do not see him anymore. I am alone in the Icefall, scared, lonely, running for my life. Concentrating, trying to cross ladders as fast as I can, I am not clipping to the ropes anymore, just holding them in my hands. Down, down, down.

Finally we are at the bottom of the Icefall. I can see the tents at Base Camp, and am relieved. It is only 10 minutes to Base Camp now. We are safe...

"Avalanche!!!" Thukten points out to the West shoulder and at the same time I hear a familiar sound. It is huge, bigger than anything we have seen here. It is moving fast toward us like an enormous growing cloud. Most likely it is going to be just snow as it reaches us, but we do not take any chances and hide behind the ice serac.

Yes, it is just snow. It covers us completely. We missed the dangerous spot by just 25 minutes or so. We are, once again, safe. Ten more minutes and we are in Base Camp. People meet and congratulate us, but their attention is not on us: "Who was still there at the avalanche spot when it came down?" All of Base Camp on their feet: "Who is missing?"

All radio frequencies are jammed: someone got hurt, but who? The Asian Trekking team is in trouble. Something is wrong within our own team. The latest news is that Bernice and Walter are lost in some crevasses and Lhakpa Sherpa is missing. We see people on the Icefall gathering at one point and not moving down the mountain. It looks like the route is broken and no one can proceed with their descent. It feels unreal.

This Everest tragedy is coming to us not from books, but from the Icefall in front of our eyes. I am terrified of what is happening. Emergency equipment is being sent up: oxygen, stretchers, down sleeping bags. No news on Lhakpa. Looks like Walter is hurt badly; he cannot move on his own, but he is alive. Bernice looks better.

40 minutes passed. We see people start moving down from the spot where they were stuck. The search for Lhakpa is in full swing, but time is running out. There is no hope anymore; too much time has passed since he disappeared. All the rescuers are in great danger; they are still at the critical spot, and another avalanche can strike at any moment. The glacier is still there, I am shaking from what is happening…

Avalanche reaches Base Camp

May 9 – Resting at Pheriche

Y esterday we left Base Camp to go down to Pheriche, located at 4200 m, for the final rest before our summit bid. This is pretty much a standard procedure for every expedition.

There are four of us. We are accompanied by Apa Sherpa – the world record holder of 18 Everest summits. His role is to make sure that we are OK, and he watches over us like a good shepherd. We take his presence for granted. It is amazing that we could talk to him at any time, hear his stories from the previous expeditions and about the people he was climbing with. This is a great opportunity and we are lucky. He is a living legend here and when people recognize him, they frequently stop to take pictures with him.

It took us almost seven hours to get down to Pheriche, including lunch and a couple of tea breaks. It was very cold, cloudy, and windy almost all the way down. I thought that I would be weak and tired after coming back from Camp 3 to Camp 2 and then to Base Camp on the two previous days, but I felt strong and moved fast. Here, at 4200 meters, there are some tiny flowers growing on the grassy spots. It is wonderful to see the flowers after all these weeks of ice. The air is thick and rich. I can run again without losing my breath.

We stay in the newly built Himalayan hotel. It is very nice and has a flushing toilet – something I have not seen for the last six weeks. I finally took a shower with hot water, and that officially completed my second rotation.

Dinner is lovely and I feel very good sitting in the warmth of the hotel, seeing people eating and talking. In this warmth and safety, the avalanche tragedy that happened only two days ago feels like it took place years ago. I love being here and the only part that is missing is that I do not have my loved ones here with me. But I feel their presence anyway. Maybe this is why I am so happy.

In the company of legendary climbers,
Pertemba Sherpa and Apa Sherpa

Pertemba Sherpa has climbed to the summit of Mt Everest three times by two different routes – along the South West Face in 1975 with Doug Scott, and again in 1979; and by the South East Ridge in 1985 with Sir Chris Bonington.
Apa Sherpa, nicknamed "Super Sherpa," holds the record for most summits of Everest with twenty one ascents as of May 2011.

May 11 – Burning Yak Poop

*I*t has been snowing here in Pheriche for two days. We now have 3 to 4 inches on the ground. It was the first morning in five weeks when we woke up and it was not a sunny day.

It is very cold in the rooms today because there is no sun. The hotels here do not have any heating system, so all inhabitants gather in the huge dining room by the stove. The dining rooms in all these hotels are built the same way. It is usually a large, about 10×20 m, room with benches around the perimeter of the room covered by soft rags.

Tables also follow the perimeter of the room, so people can sit on the benches and eat. In the middle of the room there is a metal heating stove that uses yak poop for heating. Apparently it is a very efficient fuel that produces a lot of heat, but strangely no smell. There are some chairs that surround our yak poop stove, so if you are really cold you can sit there too.

The villages here, in Khumbu Valley, are completely independent of foreign oil. Everything here runs on solar power. It is a prototype of what we might have soon in the U.S., after we get rid of our foreign oil dependency and start relying on our own inventions. I am not sure where we would get yak poop, though. Will we become dependent on foreign yak poop? This thought bothers me a lot and gives my inventive mind a lot to think about.

The Pheriche village is 300 meters long with some lodges scattered on both sides of the trail. There are no roads here because there are no cars or other mechanical transportation. There are two tiny stores in the vicinity of the hotel that we call "the Shopping Mall". We can buy candy bars there for 50% less than in the hotel. The price of a Snickers bar is around $1.20 in the Shopping Mall, and $2.50 in the hotel.

It is an entertaining experience for us to go to the Shopping Mall at least once a day to see what is on sale today. After two days of watching the sale flow and recording the price trends, I came to the conclusion that the price of candy bars here is pretty stable and does not really reflect variances of world oil prices.

Another source of entertainment is to climb a ridge right behind our hotel to reach another village that sits behind the ridge. It is called Dingbuche and you can get there in 20 minutes. Dingbuche is approximately the same size, but it has an internet cafe. The price of the connection is $40 per hour. Yes, it is expensive.

The news from Base Camp is the same. The weather is not good and some teams decided to abandon their summit bid and return from Camp 4.

Notes After

My son wrote to me that after I published this story on my blog the Google search picked it up and if you are looking for "Yak Poop" my story is the first link – I am famous on the subject!

May 14 – Summit List

*T*his is the question that I spent many days at home thinking about and preparing. What do I wear on my summit day? After this expedition I know the feeling that most men do not ever experience, but is so familiar for ladies – "I have nothing to wear!!" Seriously, it is a very important question to which I did not have an answer back home. But now it is time to make my final decision.

As the base layer I am going to wear my Patagonia base layer and long underwear, then my Patagonia R1 shirt, full body fleece OR suit, Patagonia soft shell and down suit, and OR expedition mittens. I am planning to have two relatively thin hats and use my hood in case it would not be enough. I am also taking clear goggles and sunglasses. Clear goggles will be used at night if it is too cold, or during the day time if the weather is not good. I would also need headlamps with spare batteries. I will be wearing two pair of thick wool socks with one of them adjusted with my warming system.

My climbing gear is: ice axe, crampons, harness, three carabiners, ascender, ice screw, some extra cord, and a gear sling.

In my backpack I will have spare mittens, spare goggles, spare sunglasses, thermos with a liter of tea and another liter of water in my spare mitten, limited medical supplies such as Diamox and Nifedipine, a couple of strong pills for pain, a couple of energy bars, my camera and spare batteries.

My plan is to climb to Camp 4 in my normal

climbing clothes and try not to use my down suit. I like to be a little on the cool side and not overheat. All this seems very logical now but was not clear to me before.

View of Khumbu Icefall

May 15 – Getting Sick

W hile in Pheriche, I caught a stomach bug and got sick at the end of my stay. Stomach problems are very common there because of food preparation and general hygiene. Having stomach issues is usually a serious consideration for climbers deciding to go down to the villages from Base Camp. There's a higher possibility of getting sick here after being in contact with so many trekkers and locals. Unfortunately, it happened to me too and I could not eat the last two days I was there.

I experienced diarrhea and a fever, but was not sure if a stomach problem was causing a fever or vice versa. Anyway, I decided to use all possible antibiotics I had plus the Imodium. After two days of fighting this condition I was a little better but still weak. We had no more days to recuperate. It was time to start moving to Base Camp. The climb up was very frustrating. I felt very weak, stopping frequently, instead of feeling great after resting at a lower altitude. But life is short and we have to handle whatever it presents gracefully.

Base Camp met us with beautiful sunshine and much better weather. This place felt much more like home. There were many changes on the glacier. Most of the tents now were standing tall, settled on the ice pedestals underneath them, which were created by sun melting exposed ice around the tents. I was about to take a picture of one of the tents that was towering in front of my tent when I discovered that my own tent had an even more dramatic view from the side.

I am still getting frequent chills and waking up with night sweats – all symptoms of still being sick, but I am full of hope.

Even though Base Camp feels sort of like home, it is still a very difficult place to live. It is located at 5350 meters above sea level after all! We are wearing down coats almost all the time. When I went to sleep yesterday, it was -10°C (14°F) inside my tent.

Our team is holding up pretty well in comparison to the others. According to Base Camp rumors, other teams have already lost about 25% of their members who either got sick or quit for other reasons. We are all still together except for Will Cross who decided to climb another 8000 m peak and left eight days ago.

May 16 – Experimenting with Viagra

T his was a difficult year for all the teams that came to Base Camp much earlier than our team. The weather did not cooperate and they were running out of time. As of now there were only five summits made by Sherpas who went to the summit to fix the ropes on May 5th.

We, however, are not just wasting our time here, trying to warm the ice with our own body heat. We are the real scientists now. Austrian doctors are conducting a study here. They are testing how Viagra can assist in adjusting to the high altitude and our team is gladly participating in their study. We went through the ultrasound test during which Dr. Felix measured our heart chambers. Then we took the pill and in two hours measured the heart chambers again. According to Dr. Felix our results were very good and we will use Viagra from Camp 2 and on.

Most of our conversation circles around the summit push that we are preparing for in a couple of days. We talk about how to use the oxygen masks, the optimal rates of oxygen usage and working out our summit strategies. We all get the weather forecast from the same couple of sources, so the whole Base Camp is in "short start" mode now.

It was afternoon at Base Camp and cloudy, as usual. It was the last day before going up for the Summit. We received our oxygen masks and went through the exercise of fitting them and learning how to change oxygen cylinders without blowing the regulator gaskets away. We were now fully trained and the mask felt much more comfortable than I had expected.

In the medical tent

After the sun is gone, the temperature drops fast. I am sitting in my sleeping bag with the hot water bottle inside – very nice.

May 17 – Time to Go

My alarm beeps. 3:30. I am awake in a second. This is it. We are going for it! We are leaving for Camp 2, resting for one day in-between and then continuing to Camp 3, Camp 4 and the Summit. I am excited and nervous. First things first: I take my first one liter bottle of water from my sleeping bag and gulp it down in a couple of minutes. I add my "Want More Energy" powder into my second one liter bottle and start drinking it. All is ready and packed. Last check of my gear: I am in my climbing pants already, head lamp is on me, pee bottle is packed, my thin and light down jackets are on as it is really cold now. Ice axe and crampons are outside. Snacks are packed.

I rush to the dining tent, sipping my second liter of water on the way. Pertemba Sherpa is already there meeting us with his charming smile. He knows what we are going through. He has done it many times himself and over the years has watched so many of us go up.

Breakfast is ready. I am not hungry but still trying to push my oatmeal down anyway. Nic, Krushna, and Henry are all there eating. There is not a lot of talking. We finish eating and put our harnesses on. Our Sherpas are ready too. We all go outside to pray and to take last minute pictures. We are going up! We are ready!

All of us surround our altar made out of stones at the Puja ceremony and slide deep into our thoughts. I try to calm down and think of my family. All is going to be good. I know that. Sherpas are praying and we pray with them.

Last pictures... the four of us, the first summit team from Asian Trekking 2009 Eco Everest Expedition. Henry and I take a separate picture. Henry is my "buddy", the closest friend on the team. He is strong and experienced. He will definitely make it, I am sure of it.

Leaving Base Camp for the summit

Last hugs with Dawa Steven Sherpa, our expedition leader, and Pertemba Sherpa, and we are on the way up toward the Icefall. I carry my crampons in one hand for the first 20 minutes. It is easier that way, but the ice is getting steep and I need to stop and put them on. Henry and his climbing Sherpa have already disappeared from my view. I see Nic in front of me. It is still dark and my attention is focused on listening to my breathing, trying to find some rhythm.

I am calm now, picking up some pace, bypassing Nic. I am glad that I will go through the Khumbu Icefall only two more times. Lhakpa Sherpa's tragedy is very fresh in my mind. At night the Icefall does not look as scary as during the day because I can only see the part that is directly in front of me lit up by my head lamp. But that doesn't last long since the first lights are already appearing. It is 5:00 a.m.

I make it through the Icefall in four hours and feel strong. We stop at Camp 1 for 20 minutes and melt some more ice for water. I drank 1.5 liters on the way up and plan to use another two liters before Camp 2. I know that this will make a huge difference.

It takes me another two hours to reach Camp 2. This time I feel pretty good and am not as tired as the last time. I am actually surprised at how good I feel. I try to understand the difference between today in comparison to the other day when I was struggling so much on the same stretch. I experimented with a different pattern of steps: small frequent steps or bigger, less frequent steps. To my surprise both of them worked perfectly. I maintained good pace and bypassed many climbers, staying close to my climbing partner Sherpa Thukten. All looked great.

May 18 – The Accident; Camp 2, 6400m

*I*t is a rest day and my alarm is not set. The plan is to sleep as much as possible – there are not going to be a lot of chances to sleep in the next three days.

I am awakened by loud screams and moans. I do not understand what is going on. The sounds are very strange and almost non-human. I am out of my tent as fast as I can be. It is still not possible to run at this altitude, but I see Sherpas surrounding Henry's tent and I run over there.

Henry is in his tent, moaning. His head is covered with blood, his eyes are not focused; he is looking at me, but does not see me. His climbing Sherpa is there, holding him. Other Sherpas are outside. Judging from words I am catching from them, Henry fell down outside of his tent and injured his head.

I try talk to him, but he does not respond. Finally he recognizes me, but thinks that he is at Base Camp. He does not remember what happened to him. His condition worsens. All of a sudden he starts having convulsions. I am inside of the tent holding him with all my strength, trying not to let him hit the hard floor of the tent.

Sherpas are on the radio, looking for any doctors that might be in Camp 2. Thank God, the doctor from the Russian team appears from nowhere. My Russian is helpful here and I am translating what he is saying to the Sherpas and Henry. He injects Henry with Dexamethasone and some other drugs. Then a Croatian doctor comes up from the lower parts of Camp 2 to help. She is already in contact with Base Camp medical staff – HRE. She takes over and I am relieved of my duty of holding Henry.

The Croatian doctor calmly talks to Henry and Henry talks back a little bit, and can recognize me now. He does not remember a thing about the whole accident. It is obvious that he needs to get down as soon as possible. After some resting time we help him get up on his feet. He suggests that he try to go down on his own power. Some of our team's Sherpas from Camp 2 and the Croatian doctor are going with him. They will help him to get down to Camp 1. Another group of Sherpas start up from Base Camp to meet Henry at Camp 1. They will join forces with the first group to get him down to Base Camp.

It took Sherpas 11 hours to carry Henry down to Base Camp

I give Henry my ski pole to help him walk down the ice. I am hugging him with tears in my eyes. I hope there is nothing seriously wrong with him, but it does not look good to me.

The rest of the day we all are on the radio, listening to the progress of the rescue operation. Henry collapses again somewhere below Camp 2 and they have to put him on a sled. It means that the rescue team will need to carry him down through the Icefall and all those ladders. It is going to take a very long time and a lot of effort...

The next day he was evacuated to Kathmandu by helicopter and spent some time in the hospital there. Doctors did not find anything wrong with him and eventually he was flown home. I am not a doctor, but I am pretty sure that he was having cerebral edema, lost consciousness and collapsed, hit his head against the rocks and probably got a concussion.

May 19 – Camp 3, 7200m

I am lying in my tent at Camp 3, breathing hard, and not just from the altitude. My allergies started again. I have been experiencing them for three weeks. Every time I climb up the mountain, I am fine. As soon as I come down to a camp it starts again. There is no rest for me, just a constant fight with the sneezing, blowing my nose and trying to breathe in between. My eyes are watering and I am loosing valuable moisture. I am using a roll of toilet paper as my napkin supply and it is shrinking away very fast.

All this is happening at 7200m the day before my summit day. How can I do it? I am scared and sick. Is this how it ends for me?

I am trying to use supplemental oxygen, but it does not help; the mask just complicates my nose blowing procedure. I want to quit, here and now. But how do I do that? It is so embarrassing: to get to this point faster than anyone in my team and quit. What do I do?

I need someone to talk it over with. If I go up the next day I will not take my satellite phone with me: it is extra weight. I have a good reason to call home, maybe for the last time. Oh, yes! This is good: "for the last, last time." I am now in such a "victimhood" state.

I dial home and hear my wife's voice. It's as if I was right there, in her arms. She is talking to me, asking how I am doing; telling me what is going on at home. Why doesn't she ask me to come home? This is what I need now! I am trying to complain about the allergies, but not enough to lose my pride. I can hear concerns in her lovely voice, but she is not asking me to quit. What is going on? She believes in me and trusts my judgment. I am thinking maybe I should too.

The talk is over, and I am back to my thoughts and sneezing. I have to take it one step at a time, like climbing Mt. Everest – step, after step, after step. I am calming down and trying to get some sleep. I am not scared any more. I am not a victim anymore. I am just a climber with some problems to solve. What will be here for me tomorrow?

Last ice span to Camp 3 on the steep part of the Lhotse wall

May 20 – Camp 4, 8000m

Well, well, well – I am in the "Death Zone" now at the South Col at 8000m! It looks okay though. Actually it feels very exciting. I am wearing my oxygen mask religiously with a one liter per minute rate and I am feeling great. The way to the "Death Zone" does not remind me of some of the descriptions of the near-death experiences that can be found in many books. I do not experience the "tunnel of white light"; it is actually very colorful.

Tents from multiple teams are not separated as in all other camps, but are rather located together in one large camp. There are piles of oxygen bottles near some tents ready to be taken up. Empty gas cylinders, broken tent poles, cans and other mountaineering garbage is everywhere but the place does not look dirty, just messy. This place has not been cleaned yet and the history of mountaineering equipment can be learned by browsing the garbage.

This morning we departed early from Camp 3 and continued up the Lhotse Face to gradually climb up toward the Yellow Bend (a very visible layer of yellow rocks crossing the whole face). The Bend is a relatively steep section and, at this altitude, requires good mixed (ice and rock) climbing technique to conserve energy. We have been breathing with supplemental oxygen, and the climb seemed to be no more difficult than the one before Camp 3.

Over the Yellow Bend, the route traverses the whole Lhotse Face, gaining altitude toward Geneva

Spur. Actually this is the point when we start climbing Everest, not Lhotse. I finally stopped for rest and drinks before Geneva Spur's steepest part.

The last 50 or 60 feet of the Geneva Spur are very steep. There are a lot of old ropes hanging there, so it was difficult to see which ones were new. Eventually I picked up one rope that seemed okay but tried not to load it and used mostly my legs to climb. I made a mental note to use at least two ropes on the way back to rappel down. After that steep part you are almost at Camp 4. A couple of hundred yards of an almost horizontal trail leads you to this famous place – The South Col.

Thukten and I at Camp 4

From here, you clearly can see the route up, the Balcony and the South Summit. The true summit is not visible from South Col. It is still a long way to go and Everest looks as far as the summit of Grand Teton from Jackson, Wyoming. It was 10:30am and I made it here in 4.5 hours which is not too bad.

The "normal" plan of actions is to go for the summit this evening, around 9:00 p.m. Back home I had never heard about an option of not spending the night at Camp 3 for acclimatization. But I did hear that there was an option of spending the night at Camp 4 and going for the summit not the same evening, but the next one. It was difficult for me to understand how it would be possible to go climbing again for the most difficult day of your climbing life after just a couple of hours of rest. I also knew that most people considered staying at the "Death Zone" altitude not really helpful and resting there useless.

Paul Adler, who climbed Everest in 2007 and who was the most valuable source of information for me, introduced the idea of spending an extra night at Camp 4. He also insisted that tactic was the most important decision one can make to be successful, and pointed out that Alpine Ascend International teams always spend the night at Camp 4 and they have very successful records on Everest.

Because I trusted Paul, my initial plan was also to spend the night at Camp 4. I bought extra oxygen for myself and my climbing Sherpa, and was ready to follow this plan. However, the weather forecast was such that my planned summit day of May 21 was the safest day to climb and at the last minute I decided to follow the standard procedure and climb to the summit on the same night. Also, since I climbed relatively fast, I realized that I would have much more than just a couple of hours to recuperate in Camp 4.

With 10 hours before the final summit push, I slowly walk around the South Col looking around, while carrying my backpack with the oxygen cylinder. I feel a little like a hospital patient who moves slowly along the hospital corridor pushing forward the pole with his IV line. In a couple of hours I am going to start my last preparation for the summit. I am ready and exited.

Camp 4 on South Col – The Death Zone. 8000m
The Balcony and the summit ridge are visible only from here

May 21, 2009 – The Summit, 8850m

*T*he departure time is set at 8:30 p.m., but I am starting my preparations now. I put on my two warmest pair of socks, but my feet are still a little cold. So, I turn on my electric warming system. I am all about business. Nothing extra is going on in my head, not even the usual noise of thoughts. Maybe the lack of oxygen is working its magic on me and I have enough supply only for the thoughts that I need for climbing. I remember to drink, and I do so religiously, supplying my body with the liquid that will be so valuable in the coming hours. I am ready to go, but everyone in my tent is still sleeping. I was so preoccupied with myself that I did not see that no one was preparing. What is going on? Oh, God! I mixed up the time and I am one hour early.

Finally we are ready and getting out of the tents. Thukten Sherpa is in front of me and Nima Sherpa is behind me. We plan to climb in this order so we can find each other with this climbing madness: at night all the climbers look alike wearing the down suits in just two colors: red and yellow.

Thukten starts the climb as a sprinter, jumping the rope line, unclipping from the rope and bypassing two or three people at a time. The more people we pass, the easier it is to avoid possible bottlenecks on the ropes later. I am afraid to lose him and I follow him religiously.

There is not a single negative thought in my head – not about the difficulties of the climb nor about the anxiety to get to a particular point in the climb. Breathe in, breathe out, breathe in, breathe out, then one step forward into the little light spot that is always in front of me, shining down from my head lamp. I think they call it being in the moment.

I constantly monitor my oxygen system by looking at the oxygen reservoir, a small container that looks like a beer can. It accumulates oxygen when I am breathing out and feeds it back when I am breathing in. This reservoir is made out of a clear hard plastic that protects a flexible plastic bag that inflates and deflates during the breathing cycle. I had some strange problems at Camp 4 where the inner bag was constantly inflated so I was afraid that this could happen again. When I see it inflate and deflate, I can tell that the system works.

We are constantly unclipping from the ropes and bypassing people. It takes a lot of effort, especially after I am done with each bypass. I need to stop to catch my breath for at least ten seconds. I feel very comfortable without belay during bypasses. My experience in the mixed terrain is paying back.

As the climb progresses, I lose track of time. Actually, it feels like time is collapsing. All of a sudden we are reaching the Balcony, our first stop at 8500m. This kind of time lapse has happened to me a couple of times before, when I was driving the whole night to get to Sierras. I remember looking at the mile counter and seeing that all of a sudden I just covered another 50 miles. It is the first time that I experience this during the actual climb. I am surprised that we are at the Balcony, but this thought quickly disappears from my brain. I am back inside myself, no thoughts, but full awareness of the surroundings and deep concentration.

I am sitting down at the Balcony for five minutes, drinking a little bit of water. The temperature falling to -20°C (-5°F). That is still very warm for such altitude. I see a lot of lights coming from people climbing up behind us, but there are still plenty of lights shining from much higher places on the mountain, defining the climbing path. It helps me imagine how much higher we still need to climb. I am mystified by one very particular light that is so high that I believe it is at the summit. Someone is there already.

We continue to climb, bypassing more and more people on the way. I feel good and warm, but sometimes I am really happy to be stuck behind some slow people, so I can get some rest by following their pace. I am still on my first bottle of supplemental oxygen. The climb becomes very steep (around 60 degrees) and I am worried that if I run out of oxygen here, it would be very difficult to replace my empty cylinder with a fresh one. Again, this thought disappears quickly and I am back to the darkness and breathing.

We are at the South Summit in no time. It is still dark and we are almost in front of the climbers' line. There are almost no lights in front of us. The only light very high up that I saw before is still there. It is so high that I finally realize that this is a star. I am smiling inside my mask: it is a big relief.

I know that after the South Summit the route is more exposed, potentially more dangerous. But I do not see much, I just feel the void on both sides of the ridge. Before the Hillary Step we have to traverse some steep rocks that are hanging over a 2000 m vertical drop. As we get there, I see that they do not have any visible holds for crampons. All of this is happening at almost 8800 meters while I am wearing an oxygen mask and a puffy down suit, preventing me from seeing my feet.

There were two climbers in front of us at the Hillary Step and we have to wait for at least five minutes while they get over it. I climb the Hillary Step, and am surprised that it is not difficult for me at all. However, there is a rock at the top of the Step that needs to be traversed. There is no way to do so other than to go over it as if you would climb up on a horse that is standing on the edge of a cliff opened to a 2000 meter drop.

At 4:15 am we are only 100 horizontal meters away from the summit. It is now visible in my headlight beam. I look around for any sign of dawn. But it is still completely dark, and I can only see some flashes of lightning very far on the horizon, similar to those sometimes seen from an airplane.

Nothing can stop me now! This realization comes to me for the first time and some relief goes through my body and, again, disappears as my concentration comes back.

There is a moderate wind blowing here and we are hiding behind a big rock on the side of the route and waiting for the sunrise. I am collecting some rocks to bring back as souvenirs. I am happy that I have a minute to collect them here, at the last rocky spot before the summit. There are only 4 or 5 people before us sitting on the snow slope also waiting for the sunrise.

At 4:30 we start to climb the last 100 meters up. It is

an easy climb for me. Finally we are on top of the highest mountain on the Earth, watching the sun rise! What else could anyone dream of?

My mind is still in survival mode. I experience no emotions, just observing and doing what I have to do. I look around, take pictures.

The views from the summit are spectacular. I see no sun yet, but the whole horizon is already lighting up, displaying mixtures of different colors. A thick cloud blanket covers the Earth all around us and only 8,000 meter peaks stick out from this white mantle. Lhotse and Makalu are just in front of us, Cho Oyu is to the right, and Konchenganga is very far on the horizon. Every minute more and more light is showing up and colors are changing constantly. With the first beams of sun the famous triangle shadow of Everest appears on the west. It is amazing to see its perfect lines projecting to the clouds below.

I have two cameras. Thukten Sherpa has the main camera and I have another one as a backup. He takes some pictures of me and I can see that from his position that it is not possible to take a good picture. I check his shots; they are all taken without my head or legs. I yell through my mask and ask him to leave enough distance between us to take an acceptable picture. I am not going to leave here without a good picture!

My camera goes dead after couple of shots – the lens cover is frozen and the camera reports an error – how nice! Finally we finish our photographic business and I am satisfied at least with the one of the pictures.

Thukten and I spend an hour on the summit. Nima is not here yet. We lost him on the way up. It is time for us to start our descent. At this time I see Nic approaching the summit. We hug and I take pictures for him.

Thukten and I begin our descent. I am all business again, concentrating on getting down safe and fast. My mind is so involved that I forget to turn around and look back to the summit now, at daylight.

At the top

As I remember this moment, I think about all that could have happened had I disregarded my survival concentration. I bless my focus and ability to be present to the task at hand. There is no need to regret anything, I tell myself. Maybe it is just another good reason to come back, to befriend the mountain again, to feel the power of concentration, to will myself up reaching my highest dream and find my way back, down to the safety of my home… To experience the thrill and the joy of being…

May 21 – Descent

I am coming down from the summit of Mt. Everest! How about that? In the morning light you can see how dramatic, difficult and exposed the climb is. The part of the route between the Hillary Step and South Summit goes along the huge cornices that overhang the China. These cornices have some holes in them from climbers' ice axes, so I can see China, 3000m down there. These holes are just next to my feet. I feel how strange this place is, but do not feel any worry or danger. I do not feel tired and continue going down fast.

Many people are still climbing up and we switch positions on this narrow path like zombies, behind our masks in complete silence. I am the one who unclips from the rope to bypass them and give them the advantage of staying clipped. I grab someone's down suit and use it as belay, so I can bypass them securely, without falling down 2000 meters. Some of the climbers are more conscious about this switch and are grabbing me as well, doubling the hand belay but most of them are in a trance and do not pay attention to me at all.

It is very hot. I am sweating like crazy and I hate it. At the Balcony I pull down the top portion of my down suit and wrap it around my waist. My hands are now tired from holding the endless rope that leads me down from the summit to South Col. I now see the tents of Camp 4 – just a little longer and I will be safe.

I finally reach the South Col at 8:30 a.m. I am really tired by now, but not exhausted. It is the normal fatigue from coming a long way down after a summit day. I am relaxed and dreaming. Nic is also back and I hear his loud and excited voice in the next tent. He is suggesting that we should get down to Camp 2 today. What a thought! I completely forgot that we are still at 8000m and still need to get down. Doing it that day sounds like a great idea.

We spend some time resting and rehydrating, and around 2:00 p.m. we start coming down to Camp 2. It is hard, and now I feel it. I am at the top of the Geneva Spur. There are so many ropes hanging down that I am confused which one can actually hold me. I am grabbing two of them that look new and start rappelling using both of them – just in case.

I am reaching the tents of Camp 3. Not our tents yet, but some other large group that occupies a nice shelf. There are many people there and I assume that it is the Mountain Guides group. I sit down on the snow near their tents and drink water. No one notices me. I continue down for another 20 minutes and reach our tents. Some people from our second team are there resting after their climb from Camp 2 to Camp 3. I am expecting a lot of excitement and congratulations from them, but they are all tired and somewhat subdued. I sit there, alone, outside of the tents, drinking and waiting for the sun to come down. The clouds form a spectacular view over Pumori and I take some good shoots. I am in a strange mood now. There is no more excitement or any other feelings. Just emptiness...

Around 5:00 p.m. I start coming down again. Usually people climb down the Lhotse face, protecting themselves by just holding the rope with both hands. That is how I descended from Camp 3 the first time.

This time it is a different story – I feel very exhausted and do not have any strength left in my arms. So, I decide to rappel on fixed ropes on a steep section of the Lhotse face. It is not that convenient because the lower end of each rope span is not free but anchored, still it feels much easier. Fortunately no one is climbing up nor going down. I am completely alone on the whole face. I experience a very strange feeling of isolation and loneliness, but I am not afraid.

Finally I reach the bottom of Lhotse face where the snow trail goes down at a much lower angle for another mile or so. It is foggy and hot, and I feel like I am in a dream. I cannot recognize the surroundings even though I went through this place two times during my acclimatization trips. I am completely alone here also, and now I feel scared that I lost my way. I wonder how I will find my way back in the fog.

I continue to follow an enormous amount of steps going up and down while trying to convince myself that this trail just cannot lead me to another place, because there is no "other place" here except Camp 2 somewhere down below. This very logical argument does not work very well for my tired head though.

My feet are very hot and hurting from the whole day of descending. I am constantly stopping and trying to adjust them by sticking my thin gloves somewhere inside to relieve the pressure, but it does not help. Finally at around 6:30 p.m. I reach Camp 2. It has been 36 hours of climbing without sleep: from Camp 3 to Camp 4, up to the summit and back.

Nic and I have dinner together, and I go to my tent, get into the sleeping bag, but I do not have time to zip it up. I fall into a very deep sleep.

I wake up in the middle of the night because I am very cold. What is it? I see that my sleeping bag is still open. I am zipping it up, remembering the day that just passed, smiling and falling asleep again.

In the morning it is even more difficult to move because my legs feel painfully tired after such a long decent from the summit. But the party is not over yet. I have to get to Base Camp through the Icefall for the last time. I know that I need to get down as fast as possible to avoid avalanches, but I cannot move any faster. I manage to climb down the Icefall in four hours. It is as much time as I used to climb it up and twice as long as it took me to descend the last time I was here. The final 30 minutes of the Icefall are painfully difficult, but I already see the tents and safety.

It is a very warm reception at Base Camp. Everyone congratulates me, and it is very emotional. I am thinking about the people who love me at home – my family and friends. My wife, who supported me not just throughout this whole endeavor, but also during the million times when I called for healing, moral support, or just to hear her voice. My feeling of her love and strength are not diminished by the distance that separates us. On the contrary, it is amplified by the magnitude of Everest. My sister, who was always there to help me with my multiple health related problems. My parents, who suppressed their endless fears, and supported my dream. My son and daughter who gave me the strength and desire to complete my task. To all the people who thought about me that night and followed my progress, I am so grateful.

Part 3 – Climbing Happily Ever After

I started writing this book in 2009, a couple of months after I came back from Nepal. The initial idea was to describe the expedition from the point of view of an amateur climber who climbed Everest successfully against multiple odds: age, lack of experience in high altitudes, and the overall risks of the first attempt. I wanted to share what I have learned during my many months of preparation and quest for information. I wished to create a practical guide that would tell exactly what I took with me, how I was training, what I was eating, wearing, and how I climbed Mt. Everest. My main goal was to share my experience with other climbers who wanted to embark on a similar high altitude journey.

At the time of this initial writing, I also learned that my blog was read by many people. I received many wonderful comments about how interesting it was.

Because my book idea has gradually changed and is not just a climbing guide any more, I decided to write this chapter and present some of the information that I initially planned to include for people who want to climb at high altitudes. I also believe that my perspective would be interesting to anyone who is fascinated with climbing in general. I hope that my amateur experience will give another spin to the topic that was explored many times before me, because my story is not about a tragedy on Everest – it is about success!

Blogging at Base Camp via satellite phone

From Home to Home

*A*fter the decision is made to climb Everest there really is not that much to do. You just need to lay out the plan and execute it. As for any project, the first ingredient that is required is money. For the Everest expedition you need not just money, you need a lot of money. Most North American guiding companies charge $65,000 and this price does not include your personal equipment or the flight to Nepal. There are also some other companies (mostly international ones) that charge significantly less. I am not very good with keeping spending records, but I believe that the price of getting to the Top was around $40,000 for me considering that I already had most of the equipment.

A lot of people try to raise money for such an expedition and I did too. My huge marketing effort was in general successful among my family and my friends for whose support I am very grateful. After much hard work and complicated calculations I had to take a second mortgage on my home to cover the remaining three quarters of the expenses.

So what would be a typical plan and major steps of preparation for a high altitude expedition?

- Choosing the company to climb with
- Preparing your climbing and personal equipment
- Preparing your communication equipment
- Preparing your entertainment gear

- Planning and conducting   your physical and mental training
- Arranging all your legal affairs related to the climb (insurance, tickets, etc.)

The expedition itself consists of the following major events:

1. Flying to Kathmandu

2. Flying from Kathmandu to Lukla.

After spending some time in Kathmandu your expedition will fly to Lukla. The day of this flight is usually an official start of the expedition, so you need to plan your flight from home in relation to this date.

3. Trekking to the Everest Base Camp.

You will be trekking from Lukla to the Everest Base Camp for approximately 10 days, spending nights in small lodges. During this trek we spent two nights at the same place in order to better adjust to the higher altitude.

4. Puja Ceremony.

After arriving to Base Camp you will have the Puja Ceremony. It is dedicated to a successful climb and consists of prayers to God, asking to allow you and your team to climb the mountain safely. No one usually goes up before the Puja ceremony. Some Sherpas might be working on establishing upper camps, but they would not spend nights on the mountain before the ceremony

5. The climb.

After the Puja ceremony you will start climbing the

mountain. People usually go for two or three acclimatization rotations before the summit push. With each rotation you climb higher and higher, spending between three to six or more days on every rotation.

Puja ceremony at Base Camp

6. Rest time.

After acclimatization is completed, some climbers go down to the lower altitude to recuperate before their summit push. Your rest time will depend mostly on the weather conditions. At this time you are ready and waiting for the weather "window" – the only time you can possibly reach the summit.

7. Going for the summit

When the weather forecast allows, you will be scheduled for the summit push. Usually expeditions cannot accommodate all climbers and their Sherpas in the upper camps at the same time. Because of that, your team most likely will be divided into smaller groups scheduled to climb a couple of days apart.

The summit push schedule depends on your strategy. My summit push started on May 17th when I climbed from Base Camp to Camp 2. May 18th was a rest day. I continued climbing up May 19th – Camp 2 to Camp 3; May 20th – Camp 3 to Camp 4. We started the summit attempt on the same evening of May 20th. I reached the summit on May 21st at 4:30 a.m., spending 1h15 min on the summit, and getting back to Camp 4 at 8:30 a.m. I started climbing down and reached Camp 2 on May 21st at 6:30 p.m. On May 22nd I climbed down to Base Camp. This is not a typical schedule because a lot of people come to Camp 4 much later that day and are exhausted. They spend a night there and go down to Camp 2 the following day.

8. Leaving Base Camp.

Most people leave for home from Base Camp soon after getting there, but we stayed together until May 25th, waiting for our teammates to get down from the mountain.

9. Trekking to Lukla.

After all celebrations are completed, you spend three days getting down the trek, back to Lukla.

10. Flying to Kathmandu and then back home

Climbing Route

D uring your acclimatization, the Sherpas in your team will be working on establishing four more camps. Camp 1 is at the top of Khumbu Icefall at 6100m. Camp 2 will be on the side moraine close to the Lhotse South face at 6400m. Camp 3 will be in the middle of Lhotse face between 7200m and 7400m depending on your expedition site. Camp 4 will be at the South Col at approximately 8000m.

Base Camp

Apa Sherpa and I at Base Camp. Khumbu Icefall behind us

The Everest Base Camp is built on top of Khumbu glacier that is covered with the top moraine. Sherpas, who are preparing Base Camp, build nice flat platforms out of stones and erect your expedition tents on top of them. Base Camp itself is a very large area of the glacier. It accommodates more than five hundred people. Some camps are closer to, and some are further from the so called "crampon point", the place on the glacier that leads to the famous Khumbu Icefall and where everyone is putting their crampons on.

Khumbu Icefall

As soon as you leave the crampon point, the route starts climbing up through the legendary Khumbu Icefall. For 20 to 25 min you are climbing up and down large steep ice formations without really gaining any altitude. This part of the icefall is very annoying, especially when you are coming back because you can clearly see Base Camp is very close, but still need to climb up and down for a while. After this section of the Icefall the real climb begins and you are in the heart of the renowned Khumbu Icefall.

The climb through the icefall is not technically difficult, but very dramatic. The static ropes go from the bottom to the top of the icefall and you need to be clipped to them all the time. Most people use just a sliding carabineer, not an ascender. I have to admit that even on some vertical ladders I used just a carabineer even though it did not provide very good protection. I would definitely recommend using ascender if you do not feel 100% at home out here. Sometimes I found myself skipping the clipping-on during the flat parts of the icefall in order to speed up the process. In 2009 there were around 25 – 30 ladder crossings. I was worried about this part of the climb and spent some time at home training in my backyard. You do not need to do that. Most teams practice before going to the icefall at Base Camp where it is much more convenient to practice then doing it in a backyard. And it is not that scary at all! I have not seen people fall from the ladders and most of the people I saw crossed them pretty fast.

Camp 1

Camp 1 is not really located at the top of the icefall. It is approximately 15 to 20 min from the top. There are still a lot of crevasses here, so you need to follow the path. Camp 1 is a beautiful place. You can see the whole Western Cwm in front of you and Pumori right behind you. The South Face of Lhotse shines with blue ice.

The route from Camp 1 to Camp 2 is neither difficult nor steep, but rather long. It is much longer than it looks. You still need to cross a couple of ladders here. You will see that a lot of Sherpas are leaving their crampons at Camp 1 and climb to Camp 2 without crampons. I highly recommend doing the same without leaving your crampons, but just packing them up and climbing without them. Every gram of weight that you can remove from your feet will give you much needed energy.

Camp 1. 6100m. View of Western Cwm
Lhotse in the background

Camp 2

Camp 2 is located on the side moraine approximately between 6300m and 6400m. It is actually the steepest part of the route between Camp 1 and Camp 2. Reserve your energy when you start seeing some tents of Camp 2. At this altitude it is difficult to make proper estimations regarding the climbing time. Most likely you will need another hour to get to your tents from that point.

Camp 2 is similar to Base Camp. It has large dining areas, cooks, and toilets; however it is a much colder place. It will take you at least an hour or more to get from Camp 2 to the bottom of Lhotse face where the fixed ropes start.

Camp 2, 6400m

If you are using your ski poles, as I did, you can leave them here. The wall is an ice face, mostly 45° – 65°. It is a place where your clipping technique has to be performed automatically, quickly and efficiently. Get to the anchor, clip sliding carabineer higher than the anchor and only then unclip the ascender and clip it to the new rope span. For some people it is not easy. It is important to practice this technique a lot because the "slow clipping" people are usually holding others hanging and putting everyone on the rope in danger. If you plan to wear mittens or gloves, practice your clipping techniques while you are wearing them.

Camp 3

Camp 3 is located in the middle of Lhotse Face and spaced between 7100m to 7300m on narrow platforms that are cut out of the ice.

Camp 3, 7200m

From Camp 3 the route continues up the Lhotse Face and then gradually ascends up toward the Yellow Bend – a very visible layer of yellow rocks crossing the whole face. You will be able to practice your mixed climbing skills (walking in crampons on rocks) here at the Yellow Bend. Hopefully it is not going to be a problem. At this point most of the climbers are wearing their oxygen mask, so the view of your feet is somewhat limited.

Over the Yellow Bend the route is traversing the Lhotse Face with an altitude gain toward Geneva Spur. There is a place right before the steep part of Geneva Spur where you can stop and rest. It is a good place to re-hydrate if you have not been doing it during your climb. The last 50 or 60 feet of the Geneva Spur are very steep. This part has a lot of old ropes hanging, so it is difficult to see which ones are new. Every time you see multiple ropes, try to use them for safety only, without solely relying on their protection or putting your full body weight on them. Use your legs. This is one of the rare places on the route where you will be rappelling going down. I would recommend rappelling using at least two ropes here.

After this steep part you are almost at Camp 4. A couple hundred yards of an almost horizontal trail leads you to this famous place.

Camp 4

Camp 4, a large flat place covered with rocks, is located at almost 8000m. You will see a lot of tents and oxygen piles sitting pretty close to each other. From here you can clearly see the route up, the Balcony and the South Summit. The true summit is not visible from here.

It takes 10 to 15 min to get to the beginning of the fixed ropes from your tents and then your summit climb begins. It would be dark and as with any climb at night, you will see only what is in front of you. You will see the snow, ice and mixed climbing areas before you reach the Balcony. The Balcony is a pretty wide and flat space where you can eat, drink and change your oxygen bottle if you need to.

After the Balcony the route starts climbing up to the South Summit. It is not steep in the beginning, but it becomes very steep in the last hour. On my way up I bypassed many people, but it was impossible to go around them in the last hour before the South Summit.

Walking around Camp 4. 8000m

Summit Ridge

After the South Summit you are in a very exposed part of the route. In my case it was still dark, so I did not see a lot, but I could feel the void from both sides of the ridge. For most people this part of the climb happens during the day time, so the view is very dramatic. There are some very steep rocks that you would need to traverse, but other than that it is a great place to be.

The Hillary Step is not that difficult at all, however it has a huge rock at the top hanging over the 2000m drop that you will have to traverse. The way to do it is to climb it as you would climb over a horse, facing the rocks.

Hillary Step

The Summit

After the Hillary Step you are almost there. The last hundred yards are not that steep nor exposed. It is a snow slope at about 20-25 degrees angle.

The Summit of Mt. Everest is a very small area

maybe about 12 yards wide and pretty narrow. One of the sides is covered with flags. The other side is just ice. Be careful coming to this icy side as it actually ends up as cornice hanging over China.

I spent almost 1.5 hours at the summit. I felt good and it was very early in the morning, so I enjoyed meeting a sunrise on the summit. Most people spend much less time there. Do not overestimate your strength after you summit – it is a long way back.

I am on the Mt. Everest summit. 8850m

Coming Down

It is written in many books that coming down is the most difficult and most important part. Be careful, especially before the South Summit. Most likely you will need to exchange clippings with people who are still going up. Do not hesitate to hold on to them with your hands if you are the one who is unclipped from the rope. Hold them with your hands if they need to unclip. This little support can provide much needed balance in those narrow places.

Do not forget to drink water if you still have some. On my way down it was so hot, that on the Balcony I had to pull down the upper portion of my down suit. I wished I had two separate pieces of clothing instead of a single piece suit.

One more tip here: do not forget to turn around to see the summit in a different light and at a different attitude – you have already been there! Take a lot of pictures!

I went down pretty quickly – only in three hours. This gave me a necessary rest, so I could get down to Camp 2 at the same day. If you want to do the same, make sure that you have enough energy. In case you are too tired, you can also check to see if you can have some room to spend a night at Camp 3.

Self-portrait, two days after the summit

Safety on Everest

*A*ccording to common sense, the most important aspect of any climb is to come back not just alive but with all body parts intact. How many times have we heard the stories of climbers losing their toes or fingers, dying in avalanches, lost in snow storms, or injured during falls. High altitude climbing, especially climbing of 8000m peaks, belongs to a special category. Such climbs attract many people with little or limited experiences who consider 8000m peaks something that they can climb just because they are fit and have the financial freedom to do so. The commercial nature of climbs such as Everest, Cho Oyu and some other peaks make them relatively easy to climb from an infrastructure point of view. Most companies have been doing it for many years now and have great experience with taking care of all the details. The climbers only need to pay money, stay healthy and follow their guides.

Regardless of the seemingly easy requirements for participation, people do die in such expeditions every year. I always tried to convince my mom who was very worried when I went climbing that it was safer to be in the mountains than to stay at home and possibly die in an automobile crash. I checked out some statistics and that is actually a lie. According to the facts that I found, the chance to die in auto crash in the U.S. in 2008, for instance, was 0.025%. The chance to die on Everest in a regular year is more than 1%. Oops!

So how do you protect yourself?

Moving Fast

I believe that the ability to move fast is the most important safety technique on the Everest climb. It is often necessary to pick up one's pace and move significantly faster over some spans with high exposure to avalanches or other hazards. Khumbu Icefall is such a place. You do not want to spend extra time there. It is especially true on descent. People most likely descend Icefall at a time when the sun is up and the ice is melting because they usually start from Camp 2 bypassing Camp 1 on the way down, after which the Icefall starts. On the same day the avalanche killed Lhakpa Sherpa, a member of our team, I was also descending from Camp 2 to Base Camp. I was lucky enough to miss the avalanche by 25 minutes or so. It was very hot. Thukten felt the danger and was running down so fast that I could not see him for a long time. I was also concerned with the hot temperature and was going down much faster than I normally would. This saved my life.

Because of the multi-day nature of the climb it is also very important to generally reduce time on the mountain between camps. Coming to the next camp as early as possible gives you more time to recover and re-hydrate before the next day. For instance, it is essential to come to Camp 4 early, because the summit attempt starts the same evening. By reducing overall time between camps, you will be climbing in more comfortable temperatures and lessen the sun exposure. You will also be able to re-hydrate faster at camps where more water is available.

Moving fast also means pacing yourself. Some climbers do not have experience with pacing their activities at this altitude. They start very fast and then slow their pace so much that the overall time between camps is exceptionally long. From my experience, pacing at such altitudes is much more difficult than during a "normal" altitude climb. For instance, gaining 3000 feet (1000 m) of altitude between 11,000 feet and 14,100 feet is very different then gaining the same 3000 feet of altitude between 20,000 feet and 23,000 feet.

On my second rotation, for example, when I was climbing from Base Camp to Camp 2 directly, I crossed the Icefall in 4 hours 30 minutes and then struggled for three more hours to Camp 2. I might have been better off spending 30 minutes more on the Icefall and shortening my time between Camp 1 and Camp 2. By doing so I would come to Camp 2 less exhausted.

Pacing yourself on the descent is also very important. I remember my first time coming down from Camp 3 on Lhotse Face. I felt pretty comfortable on ice and the whole descent for me was not technically difficult. I started going down very fast, bypassing people on the way, and found myself completely out of breath at the bergschrund. I could not recover for a long time. Generally speaking, when Everest climbers spend more than six hours in between camps, they are definitely struggling.

Using Fixed Ropes

Another important issue that affects safety of not just a single climber, but everyone on the Everest route is an incorrect usage of static or fixed ropes. These ropes provide the only marginal safety on the slopes of the Lhotse Face and above. Many climbers are clipped to them at the same time and often even on the same rope span between anchors.

Climbers with less experience tend to put too much of their weight on the ropes instead of using them just as a safety line and move mostly with their own feet. Such poor climbing technique is tiring and also puts everyone in danger in case the rope comes apart because of the load.

Climbers with less experience also tend to spend longer switching safety carabiners or ascenders near anchors. The lack of such experience does not allow them to do that fast enough with their gloves on, and they do not feel comfortable taking their gloves off because they do not know when that can be done safely.

Hydration

Proper hydration is imperative on any climb, but it is crucial at Everest's altitudes. Most climbers on Everest usually carry one to two liters of water between camps. I believe it is completely unacceptable and at least three liters have to be used between camps. I was the most efficient and strong on the days when I drank two liters between Base Camp and Camp 1, then one liter at Camp 1, where we spent 30 minutes just to re-hydrate, and then another 1.5 liters of water between Camp 1 and Camp 2. Climbers usually carry very little weight between camps and one extra liter of water would not make a big difference on the overall weight, but could make a huge difference in their performance.

Another aspect of hydration is drinking water

before the climb. When it was possible, I had the following water routine that I used on the trek, as well as the whole climb. I would fill up two of the one liter bottles with (boiled) hot water before I went to bed. On the trek it was the same water we used to prepare our tea or coffee so it was safe to drink. I would use these two bottles to warm up in my sleeping bag and drink some of it during the night. In the morning they would reach sleeping bag temperature, so I could easily drink one liter while still in my sleeping bag. My rule was not to get out of the sleeping bag until I drank a liter of water.

Some people have difficulties drinking water that is not cold. I actually prefer drinking water at room temperature, not because I like it, but because I can drink a lot of it fast. It does not taste very good and I often forced myself to do so, but this was in line with the climbing mountains – going through the struggle. I would drink my second liter during my morning chores and before the climb started.

Proper layering

It is known that a proper layering system allows you to feel more comfortable and not lose too much water to perspiration. The latter is crucial on the Everest climb where the climb can be very hot during the sunniest part of the day and the temperature can change dramatically in a matter of seconds. I am not sure how other people's thermoregulation works, but my body system hates Gore-Tex and I suspect that I am not that unique in that. Gore-Tex does not breathe (of course it breathes during company experiments and in advertisement brochures, but in my opinion, not in real world conditions). Most of the climbers that I have seen were wearing Gore-Tex and I suspect many of them were struggling with perspiration. Unless it is raining or snowing with wet snow I won't wear it. Ideally you have to function on Everest without sweating. Sometimes it is almost impossible with 100 degrees Fahrenheit temperatures and no wind, but this is another reason to get up early and move fast.

My rules are:
- If I start climbing and do not feel chilly I am already overdressed.
- If I feel even a little hot, I will stop and take off some layers.
- I always have enough layers with me to survive a nasty storm at any altitude, regardless of how nice the weather is when I start.

Prepare for the unexpected

Before you go to Mt. Everest, you need to be able to answer a number of questions:

- Are you ready to fight for your survival 100% if something goes wrong?
- Are you ready to face a snow storm that hits you in the face in the Western Cwm after long hours of climbing, even when exhausted?
- Do you have enough experience to go through the heavily crevassed glacier, roped up, at 6200m, when the whole route is hidden?
- Can you find your way through alone without falling into the crevasse?
- Can you hold your partner and rescue him from

the crevasse if an accident happens?

There was a Kazakh team in 2009 that stayed on the mountain during the snow storm that started on May 25. After the storm the whole Icefall route was covered with snow. They spent 15 hours looking for the way down instead of the normal two hours. Safety comes with practice and experience, and that is what is needed on Everest.

Monitoring your conditions and state of mind

During the Everest climb, you need to be able to monitor your conditions and state of mind. It is hard to know how it feels if you do not have an adequate experience. You need to know your reserves.

The altitude speeds up all processes in your body. If you get sick, the sickness progresses very fast. You need to be able to recognize that you are sick and do something about it immediately. Most likely you would need to get down. If you do not take care of your illness, you will be putting not only yourself in danger, but other people around you who would be forced to take care of you once your illness develops.

You will also need to recognize if you begin having problems thinking straight and making right decisions. During my summit day, for instance, I definitely lost track of time. Everything seemed to be happening very fast. All of a sudden we were at the Balcony, then at the South Summit. Analyzing my conditions now, I think that I was possibly losing my sense of reality. I was also unusually concerned with monitoring my conditions – especially breathing. But if I did not function properly, I would probably be acting the opposite way and not be concerned with such monitoring at all.

Other aspects of monitoring include letting your teammates know what is going on with you. It is not a place for being macho. One of our expedition members was taking some prescription drugs that were erroneously recommended for him by his doctor back in the U.S. He did not tell anyone what he was taking, even though this particular drug is commonly used for emergencies at high altitude and was frequently discussed during our conversations. Just before the summit day he felt really sick and only then did we discover that he was taking this drug. He was literally saved by an emergency evacuation to Kathmandu.

Knowing medical implications

The story about inappropriate usage of medications leads to a very important point. You have to know what kind of medical emergencies could happen at the high altitude and be adequately educated about how to deal with them. You need to become familiar with not just the altitude related sicknesses, but also know how to take care of common medical issues such as cold, flu and stomach problems. Anything can happen to you on a mountain and a doctor most likely will not be available. Even though your group might include a doctor and Base Camp has an HRA unit, it is best for you to know how you can take care of yourself and what to do or not do in case you are sick. All this information is available through books, as well as the web.

Do not over-rely on guides and their knowledge

Even though you might be a participant of a guided expedition, it is still useful (and really cool) to be self-reliant regardless of who takes care of you on the mountain. Guides in your expedition are there to guide you, not rescue you. Definitely they will try to rescue you if something goes wrong, but your goal is not to get in such situations. I spoke with some people who successfully climbed Everest before me. I was interested in their oxygen tactic, oxygen flow rates, where cylinders were exchanged, etc. However, some of the climbers that were part of the guided group could not remember any such information. All their oxygen was arranged for them and all rates were adjusted by their guides or Sherpas.

By not knowing such vital information you put yourself in danger because you are not prepared to make a life and death decision if needed. You basically hand over your life to someone else. Guides are very valuable resources of experience and information. It is wise to use your time and money to learn as much as you can from them and become as self-sufficient as possible.

Acclimatization Tactics

There are multiple considerations that make acclimatization tactics on Everest not a trivial topic. The goal of the acclimatization time is to gain maximum adaptation to the altitude with minimum loss of energy.

The second major consideration on the South side of Everest is the Khumbu Icefall. As it is the most dangerous place on the route, you want to minimize your exposure to this part of the route. What are the options there?

To reduce the number of trips through the icefall, some teams go to another mountain before they come to Base Camp. Our Austrian group, that operated on their own, but was also a part of our Everest Eco Expedition 2009, went for acclimatization to Island Peak. I am not sure that I agree with this tactic. Island Peak is 20,305 ft. which is only 3000ft higher than Base Camp. Climbing to Island Peak summit but without sleeping there, you just add a very short exposure to 20,000ft. I did not see that the Austrian climbers were much more prepared for our first trip to Camp 1 in comparison to the rest of the team who did not climb Island Peak. I see their point though – it was another peak to climb.

Another major question is to sleep at Camp 3 or not. Many climbers on the last rotation before the summit bid go to Camp 3, but do not sleep there. The night at Camp 3 without oxygen is considered a brutal experience, so some people chose not to stay there overnight. However, skipping the night at this altitude definitely reduces your acclimatization preparation, so these climbers are much more dependent on the supplemental oxygen in comparison to others who slept at Camp 3 without oxygen. One has to realize that dependence on supplemental oxygen reduces your safety margin. If something goes wrong on the summit day, your ability to move (presumably down) without oxygen can save your life.

One of our team members had a problem with his oxygen mask near the Balcony – it just froze. He was forced to go down without oxygen even though he had plenty of full cylinders and Sherpa's support.

In my opinion, sleeping at Camp 3 gives you maximum acclimatization and also is a good test of your mental readiness to continue.

Most guided groups implement three rotations before their summit bid. The first rotation is to Camp 1 and back to Base Camp, the second rotation is to Camp 2 and back, and the third one is to Camp 3 and back.

The following is my acclimatization tactic.

First and foremost, I was very happy that we spent two more days trekking to Base Camp than most of the teams. You cannot force your body to adapt fast to the altitude, so spending time walking around Khumbu valley is time very well spent.

The second major approach was not to rush to leave Base Camp for the first rotation. I spent another five days at Base Camp before we started climbing.

I decided that my major barometer would be my body. I would not commit to two or three rotation trips beforehand, but rather decided to watch myself and make future choices based on my condition. I intended to go to Camp 1 and spend the night there. If all was good, I would continue to Camp 2 the next day. If I did not feel well at Camp 1, I would stay for another night and observe my acclimatization. If I felt really bad, I would go down the next day. This was my plan.

After spending a night at Camp 1 I felt pretty good and the next day went to Camp 2. I spent two nights at Camp 2, but suddenly the morning after my second night I did not feel good: I felt dizzy and could not eat. I got scared and decided to descend. When I got to Camp 1 and sat down to drink, I felt much better. I continued monitoring my condition and because I felt much better, I decided to stay at Camp 1 for another night. This was a good decision as it gave me another night at an altitude much higher than Base Camp. On my first rotation I spent four nights at higher altitude: two at Camp 1 and two at Camp 2.

On my second rotation I went to Camp 2 directly, without stopping at Camp 1. This was a standard tactic because Camp 1 is usually used for the first rotation and then for emergencies only. I was still not sure if I would be sleeping at Camp 3. I was following my tactics of watching my condition and making decisions based on how I felt. I spent two nights at Camp 2 and went for Camp 3 the next morning. My plan was to spend at least a full day at Camp 3 before deciding upon descending or sleeping out there. As the day progressed I felt good and decided to stay for the night. I actually spent a very good night at Camp 3 and did not regret my decision.

As soon as you have slept at Camp 3 you are ready for the summit. My second rotation was the last one before the summit push.

Another standard procedure before the summit is

to go down to the lower altitude to recuperate. We went to Pheriche and were planning to spend 4 days out there. Unfortunately, the weather was not good and we spent seven days at Pheriche and two more days coming back to Base Camp. It is hard to estimate how much this approach helps your body, but it has been done for years and you just have to trust it. Do not try to get to Base Camp in one day – It does not make sense to rest for a few days and then force yourself for a one day sprint.

The last question is whether to spend one extra night at Camp 4. The "normal" behavior is to go from Camp 3 to Camp 4 in the morning and continue your climb to the summit on the same day starting around 9 p.m. The alternative is to spend a night there and go for the summit the next evening.

From my experience and also an experience of Bill Burke (my team member and the oldest American who reached the summit at age 67) I can suggest the following. If you are a slow climber and might need more than 6 hours to reach Camp 4, staying there for another night makes a lot of sense and definitely increases your chances of success. Bill did exactly that.

Supplemental Oxygen

How much supplemental oxygen do you need?

What is the oxygen rate to use and when?

Do you need to buy extra bottles?

I had all these questions before the expedition and they were discussed multiple times during our dinners on the mountains. Most of the companies provide five four-liter bottles of oxygen that are included in the expedition price. You also have an option to buy more if you want. The standard plan is to use these five bottles as follows:

You start using the first bottle at night at Camp 3 and continue using it while climbing to Camp 4.

You use the second bottle during the day at Camp 4 and leave it there.

The third bottle is used to reach the Balcony. The fourth is used from the Balcony to the Summit and is switched for the last one at the summit or on the South summit. The last bottle is used to get down and spend the night at Camp 4.

Now let's talk about the rates and how long each bottle can last. I am going to start with the formulas, so you can make your own calculation, according to your specifics.

The formula that we use to get the number of minutes the bottle will last was to multiply the volume of the bottle by the pressure in the bottle and divide by the rate of use.

For instance, four-liter bottles with the pressure of 300bar and the rate of use at two liters per minute will last:

4x300/2=600min or 10 hours.

We used the POISK system oxygen bottles that are the most common on Everest. The system comes with three or four-liter bottles. According to the POISK specification the pressure in each bottle is 320 bar at a temperature of +20°C. However, I can guarantee that you will not climb Everest at this temperature. It will actually be around -25°C or lower. At this temperature the pressure in your bottle will lose around 15%. You also have to take into account the fact that not all bottles are made equal and take another 5% off. To be safe, we will consider the pressure in your bottle as being 80% of the nominal which is 250 bars.

The next step is to multiply bottle pressure by the bottle volume:

A four-liter bottle will hold 4x250=1,000L of oxygen

If you are using 2L/min (liter per minute) rate, this bottle will last for 1,000/2=500 minutes which is 8.3 hours.

If your rate is 3 L/min, it will last for 1,000/3=333 minutes which is 5.5 hours.

After all calculations you can see your estimations in the following table that reflects hours of usage:

Rate	1L/min	2L/min	3L/min	4L/min
3L Bottle	12h	6.2h	4.1h	3.1h
4L Bottle	16	8.3h	5.5h	4.1h

I started using supplemental oxygen on my summit bid during the night in Camp 3. It was a 3L bottle and I used 1L/min. I used this bottle for 6 or 7 hours during the night and used the rest of it getting up to Camp 4 with the rate of 1.5L/min. Because I climbed pretty fast, it was enough for me. Most of the teams now are using 4L bottles, so you can calculate your oxygen needs accordingly. I started using my second 3L bottle at Camp 4 with the rate of 1L/min and continued using it until we left at 9:00 p.m. for the summit. I left this second bottle in my tent.

My first climbing summit bottle was 4L and I started it at 2.5L/min. I felt great and was climbing very fast, bypassing many climbers on the way. I changed this bottle only at the South Summit.

Using supplemental oxygen at Camp 4

I changed to a new 3L bottle on the South Summit and it lasted me through the summit and back to the South Summit again. I used my third 3L bottle to get back to South Col, rest there for four hours and get down to Camp 2 the same day. Basically, I used only one 4L bottle and 1.5 3L bottles from Camp 4 through the summit and back to Camp 2.

Depending on your state and goals, you will have to make a decision there. You can use a slightly higher flow rate and move faster, or you can use a slower oxygen rate and move slower. I decided to do the former, as I believe moving faster is much safer. It is also difficult to discern how fast or slow you move. In my case, I knew that I was moving fast because I was bypassing other climbers. From my experience, not many people use this technique because it requires unclipping from the ropes on the steep sections. If you do not consider this method, I would recommend conserving the oxygen by using slower flow rates because your pace might be contingent on the pace of the people in front of you.

Staying Healthy

S taying healthy is the most important aspect of a successful expedition, and because of the length of the expedition and the harsh conditions, this is not a trivial task. You could be in the best shape of your life, the weather could be perfect, but if you get sick you are not going anywhere.

Also, the most important task is to be healthy at the right moment, before the summit push. That means that if you got sick at some point you have to be smart about how to get well quickly. Sometimes it means going down or at least not going up.

There are multiple aspects of maintaining health and to be in your top physical form on the mountain.

Coming to Nepal

It all starts on the airplane that brings you to Nepal. You are going to travel many hours inside that enclosed space with many people. I brought medical surgical masks with me that I started using on the airplane. Do not be embarrassed. Sometimes you can see that some people do that on planes. They come from countries where air is not as clean as in the U.S. and they do not falter to use masks. Also, do not hesitate to get up from your seat and wash your hands before the meal. I kept a pack of wipes with me and used them before each meal.

Your next possible place of catching an illness is Katmandu. You would be amazed how dirty the air in this city is. In addition to being very interesting and colorful, Kathmandu is extremely polluted and dusty.

Most likely you will be staying in a good hotel that your expedition company provides for you at Kathmandu before the climb. If you can, try to postpone all sightseeing until after the climb. The best thing to do is to arrive in Kathmandu just before your flight to Lukla. Even if you need to buy something in Kathmandu, you do not need more than a day to take care of your shopping.

It is important to eat only in good restaurants and do not buy any food on the streets in Kathmandu. Wash your hands regularly and use a sanitizer whenever possible. Do not drink any water in the city except from unopened bottles. If you go shopping or sightseeing, do not hesitate to use your dust mask – You will see many local people do that as well.

Food

On the trek you mainly have a danger of getting sick from food poisoning or contracting a virus from other sick people who are staying in hotels. Use common sense and use hands sanitizer as much as possible. Do not eat any food such as popcorn if you see that someone is eating it with their hands. You can discuss with your teammates using spare cups to distribute things such as popcorn if need be.

Food poisoning is a real danger on the trek. If you get sick, start using a corresponding antibiotic immediately. Do not wait to see how it will progress as you might do at home. Here if you are late with your decision, you may have to go home to recover.

Sun Exposure

Sun exposure at such high altitudes is another factor that can influence your success. I usually grow my beard while in expedition, so I have at least part of my face protected. Of course you will use sun block. Just remember that you need to cover such areas as the inside of your nose, your ears and especially your lips. I managed to get through the whole expedition without a single sunburn.

The Khumbu Cough

Many climbers in the Everest expeditions experience the so called Khumbu cough. You may have read some stories about people breaking their ribs from such a cough.

Protecting from dust and sun

The cause of it is usually claimed to be related to

the cold and dry air up in the mountains. It is probably true, but I also believe that many people get it from the pollution in Kathmandu or inhaling dust during the trek. You cannot recover from it at the high altitude. As previously suggested, use your face mask or buffs. It was hard for me to use masks especially when it was hot and I was going up the hill. Try to find masks that have an exhaust valve. They can be found at most hardware stores. The valve allows hot air from your breath to escape easily. These masks are not cheap, but your expedition and health are much more expensive. As an alternative to the mask, many people use buffs. The reason I prefer a mask is because they are disposable. I do not remember hearing any coughing from the members of our expedition because all of us were experienced climbers and everyone was aware of the danger.

I was also using Psolar face masks. You can look them up online. They all have a heat/moisture exchanger that captures heat and moisture when you exhale, as well as warms up and moisturizes your air when you inhale. I actually used such system first during my Denali climb in 2007. I was wearing the Psolar HX helmet Balaclava during my summit day on Denali and it served me well.

During our descent we got into a storm and some of my teammates got frostbites. My face was covered with this mask and goggles, so I was okay. On Everest, in addition to HX Balaclava I bought lightweight Psolar EX Facemask. I found that the Balaclava was too warm for me at Base Camp and not really versatile enough. On the summit day it could not be worn as I was also wearing the oxygen mask. I still could use my hat with the face mask which together worked like a Balaclava.

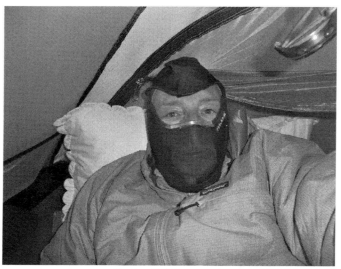

Psolar EX face mask

I found that the face mask design had some flaws. It felt like whoever designed it never tried to use it themselves. It was always sliding down from the back of my head, so I had to sew two little elastic straps to go over the top of my head and hold the mask in place. The other small, but very annoying detail was the piece of Velcro that hooked the mask at the back of the head. It was touching and hurting my neck because the Velcro material is very stiff. Try your mask at home and check how it fits you. You might need to add a little piece of neoprene fleece to protect your skin and make sure the mask does not hurt you.

Some people can sleep using this face mask. I could

not. I used it when I was laying in my tent entertaining myself by watching movies on my player a couple of hours a day. That was all I needed to prevent coughing. I also carried this mask with me all the time when I went to upper camps – in case I needed protection from a storm.

Sometimes at Base Camp when I felt my throat was a bit irritated, I covered myself with a towel and inhaled steam from a bowl of boiled water mixed with a couple of drops of healing oils that Sherpas brought with them. It worked like magic on me and only took 5-10 minutes.

Altitude

You will find in mountaineering literature that the description of very high altitude is an elevation between 3500 – 5500 m (11,500 – 18,000 ft.) and everything that is higher than that is considered to be an extreme altitude. Congratulations! For five or six weeks you will be living and climbing at the extreme altitude.

A lot of my anticipation of Everest extreme altitude came from reading books and, especially, Jon Krakauer's book "Into thin air". You might remember detailed descriptions of his headaches, vomiting and more. I did not have any of these nor did I see a lot of these actions from my teammates. All these sensations are individual and hopefully you will also not experience such conditions. However, you have to stay very vigilant and monitor yourself.

What I did experience was a so called chain stroke breathing that is sometimes called periodic breathing. It is a phenomenon that many of my teammates experienced as well. You can find scientific explanation of these conditions online. I just want to mention that the first time I went through this, it was a scary moment especially because it comes at night after you fall asleep. I had this condition three times during my trip and each time it would last for some hours. The first time it was in my first night at Camp 1 and two times at Camp 2. What was interesting is that I did not have it at the night I spent at Camp 3. I relate this to the fact that at Camp 3 I was very conscious about my pressure breathing the whole day until I went to sleep

Just being aware of these possible problems will help you to try to be calmer about it, taking it as something that is part of your life here at altitude. Try to find this condition entertaining and watch it as if it was not happening to you. You are not alone and it is not that dangerous.

How did I avoid altitude problems? As I said, I did not have a single headache or vomiting whatsoever. It might be related to the preventative measures I describe below or I might just be lucky to have such genetics, or a combination of both. I knew that I had no problems with altitude on Mt. Denali and usually would not have any problems during my short climbs where I would go from 0 to 12,000 feet in one day. Nevertheless, I did not take any chances in this regard. I made it my goal to be constantly aware of the altitude and act accordingly.

First and most importantly, I was drinking enough water. I followed my water routine religiously. There is no limit of how much you should drink, – just make sure you have a pee bottle with you. To facilitate my water drinking I usually added some powder, similar to sport drinks flavoring, to my water that made it a little tastier. For me this was a big factor in being able to easily drink much more liquid.

As a climber living in Chicago and climbing only on long weekends, I was using Diamox (Acetazolamide) to adjust to the altitude faster. Diamox stimulates deeper breathing at night. I usually took 125 mg before going to bed every time I had to sleep at a new altitude. I do not know if Diamox had an effect on me or I felt better because of the placebo effect, but it does not really matter. It helped me a lot. Some people have slight side effects from Diamox such as tingling in their fingers, but I did not.

On Everest I was also using Ginkgo Biloba – a supplement that is also claimed to be helpful at high altitude. Again, I cannot support this statement with my personal scientific facts about its usefulness, but it will not hurt you in my opinion. My thinking was – use all you can if it does not hurt you.

Pressure breathing is also a technique that I was trying to use religiously at high altitudes. It is very simple – all you need to do is purse your lips together and exhaling forcefully through your mouth. It is a known fact that as soon as you stop moving, your heart and breathing rates slows down. Breathing shallower or slower will lower the oxygen concentration in your blood causing the oxygen starvation in your body. The danger is especially high during the rest stops, time spent in camps and nights because during your moving periods you are breathing hard anyway. That is why novice climbers are always advised to do something while in camps and avoid laying down or falling asleep. During all my stops I was trying to remember that and continue my pressure breathing. I believe that was the reason I did not have a problem with periodic breathing at Camp 3.

The space in Camp 3 is so limited that you cannot do anything except stand outside of the tent or lie inside of the tent. I have read many accounts where people consider the night at Camp 3 without supplemental oxygen as the hardest. Most people do not sleep well at Camp 3. They mostly feel cold there, but not from the ambient temperature. Rather, it is the lack of oxygen in their body. Being aware of my limited movement, I was constantly using pressure breathing during the whole day at Camp 3 which allowed me to spend the night fairly comfortably, not being cold and sleeping without any problems. It was a good night despite the allergies that bothered me there.

Many climbers take baby aspirin as a measure of preventing blood thickening problems from developing due to the higher rate of hemoglobin. I tried to do that as well, but was not very consistent about it.

Snow Blindness

Snow blindness is a real danger on Everest. On summit day you will start your climb at night and you might not be wearing goggles just as I was not wearing them. You might be climbing for seven to eight hours before the sun comes out, but at sunrise you might not get a moment to stop and get your sunglasses out. Most climbers are familiar with the fact that the sun reflection from the snow can burn your corneas. At extreme altitude, because of thin air this can happen in a matter of minutes. When I met the sunrise on the summit, it was not that bright initially. Fortunately, I remembered to get my sunglasses out, but Thukten did not. I reminded him about that and I remember that he was very grateful. Watch out for your friends and ask them to watch out for your safety as well.

There is another annoying thing that might happen on your way down, when you are watching your feet, and your head is hanging down. Your glasses become foggy when you breathe out wearing an oxygen mask. I did not have this problem, but I've heard about other people's problems and want to point out how this can be very dangerous. At the time of the climb your brain does not function very well, so you need to be careful about not taking your sun glasses off, even if keeping them on irritates you. Wearing goggles would solve the problem. However, you might find yourself sweating as soon as the sun hits the snow and wearing goggles would add to overall over-heating. By the way, if you are wearing a separate down parka and down pants versus a full body down suit, you can take the parka off and stay dry all the time. The last thing to remember is that even if there is no open sun exposure, the invisible sun rays can still be very harmful to your eyes.

Recovering after sickness

As previously mentioned, it is much more difficult to recover from sickness at high altitudes. If you get sick during the trek, I advise you to not continue moving up the trek. Stay at the tea house for a couple of days and get better first. Then you will be ready to continue moving up. It is easier to get better at the lower altitude. Do not be afraid to stay behind your teammates. The winner is not the one who gets to Base Camp the fastest, but rather the one who gets to the top. You will have plenty of time to catch up.

If you get sick higher on the mountain – go down to Base Camp. If it is something serious, consider getting down even lower. For example, one of the members of our expedition felt a toothache after being at Base Camp for some time. He did not have a chance to go up to the mountains yet, but he was forced to go down to Namche Bazaar for extraction. He spent almost a week doing this round trip, but he still managed to get back to the acclimatization schedule and was ready for the summit attempt on time.

It is very important to trust in your ability to recover if you get sick. Before the summit push we went down to Pheriche for four days. We ended up staying there for eight days because the weather forecast was bad and we could not go for the summit push. Two days before going back to Base Camp I became ill with both fever and diarrhea. I was pretty upset because I felt good for six weeks and got sick at the most crucial moment of my expedition. I started taking care of myself immediately using all relevant medications I had in reserve. I managed to stop my diarrhea in one day, but my fever lasted for two days. I am usually very much affected by even a low fever and this time was no exception. I felt weak walking even at 4200 m in Pheriche.

Then we had to move up and I could not stay any longer at Pheriche. We were too far in the Everest game, so I left. The next two days of trekking to Base Camp were very difficult for me. Instead of feeling my best before the summit bid, I was feeling my worst. Even though I was upset, I did not lose my trust and optimism. I knew that I would get better and be ready for the summit. I continued my recovery routine, feeling better and better every day. After two days in Base Camp I felt as strong as before.

Oximeter

To monitor my oxygen saturation, I brought a small finger Oximeter with me. My oxygen saturation was around 80 (norm is 100) when I came to Base Camp for the first time and it was around 92 before I left. I specifically did not take it higher than Base Camp. I was afraid to see the low numbers and then start feeling bad because of what I saw. Our mind is a very powerful instrument and it does not always work to our advantage. I decided to fully rely on my sensations especially because these measurements are objective and there is no right or wrong number at such altitude. I saw that even Sherpas do not have high oxygen saturation at high altitudes. However, this instrument might be helpful in case you are feeling bad. The oxygen saturation might be so low that as to be an indication you need to make an emergency descent.

Part 4 – Confessions of a Climber's Wife

*A*n important aspect of my preparation was my mental training, provided by my wife Svetlana (Lana) Pritzker, who specializes in mind/body connection and present moment centered awareness. She is Life Purpose Intuitive, a Transformational Coach and inspiring mentor for many people who come to her sessions and seminars. She is always at the forefront of new discoveries in the field of consciousness, a role model who uplifts and motivates people to know, love and fulfill their dreams

I was going to write in detail about my training, meditations and working with her before the expedition. I thought that such information would be very helpful, not only for athletes but definitely for everybody else as well. As I started to write this chapter, I soon realized that even though I understood concepts and could do a lot of things that she taught me, I couldn't write about them with precision and richness that she would. Then I got an idea. What if I conducted an interview with her, recorded it and then transcribed it for the book.

So we went for a walk around our neighborhood with the voice recorder and I asked her all kinds of questions that I encountered during our talks. Very soon I found that I liked my reporter's role and started exploring other controversial topics (as a good reporter would do), such as one's family's attitude toward extreme sports and climbing in particular.

It was almost two hours of attention-grabbing and practical conversation. When we transcribed it, we ended up with almost forty standard size pages. It was a book on its own.

At Namche Bazaar

After careful consideration and multiple editing, we decided to include only a small part of the interview which is presented in this chapter. We made a decision to refer readers who are interested in Svetlana's teachings, to her web site[1], to the multiple articles she's written for Your Tango[2], online magazine about relating, and to more than 80 of her videos on YouTube (Lana Pritzker channel). Or you can just use Google for Svetlana Pritzker and you will not be disappointed.

High Altitude – The Ultimate Survival Test

You've been the wife of a climber, and you've trekked to Base Camp of Mount Everest yourself. What do you think about climbing in general and especially about climbing at high altitudes, which requires special skills and training to survive in such extreme conditions?

Well, this is a very interesting question. I believe that as long as we live, we test ourselves by exploring our ability to survive. Each of us has a unique way to express this desire physically, accessing high levels of vitality, valor and strength. People go for all kinds of experiences to elicit the feeling of expansion and perform at their peak potential. At the same time, this desire should not be mistaken for the need to prove to yourself or to prove to others your own worthiness.

Just like it was for you, everything starts with an idea, with a dream. Without dreams, we are pretty much all about eating, sleeping, and procreating. This level of existence is common and normal. There is

---

[1] www.energy4action.com

[2] www.yourtango.com/experts/lanapritzker

nothing to be ashamed of or to judge. We find a great level of entertainment, satisfaction, and fulfillment living in this realm of existence. Once you satisfy your basic needs and have a strong foundation for surviving at the basic level, you move on to the next level – the realm of personal growth where you find some interesting things to explore, in addition to satisfying your everyday needs.

When somebody dreams about climbing Mount Everest, it is almost as if they are connecting to the huge morphic field of EVEREST that has been energetically charged by all the people who ever thought about it, saw the movies, read the books, or connected to the idea that they can be part of it. Climbers who embarked on this journey in the past – when none of the technologies of today were available – have opened the door into the new reality of human existence. Today's climbers are standing on their shoulders, connecting to giant dreams and accomplishments, and offering their own commitment and courage to set an example for those who will be climbing Mt. Everest in the future.

Climbing Mt. Everest is about becoming a link in a long chain of human accomplishments, courage, self-fulfillment, camaraderie, and bravery. When you are there, climbing the mountain, you are not just you. You are also a part of everything else that has happened there before and whatever will be there after you are gone. Without you, a link in this chain, the Everest story, is not complete. You are like a piece of a human puzzle that fits perfectly there, no matter where you find yourself in this experience. Whether you successfully completed the summit or successfully turned back, respecting your limitations and the power of the mountain, this experience leaves a very strong imprint on your whole life because of all these connections that were made before, during, and after your climb.

I believe that every climber who thinks of climbing any high altitude mountain, Everest especially because it is such a famous, sought after and challenging mountain, brings back home a piece of the higher self that is priceless. When you reach your peak potential and connect with the bigger part of yourself that guides you there and helps you survive in such extreme conditions, your life and the lives of those that partake in your experience are changed forever.

Dreaming Big

W hat do you think about dreams that seem impossible to fulfill?

If achieving a dream would be an easy target, you would not call it a dream. You would simply do what you wish and go on fulfilling your next desire. The dream by definition is a fantasy, an idea that speaks to you, yet seems unreachable in the moment. At the same time, when you have a dream, your desire to fulfill it is beginning to unfold this possibility into a reality that is your true destiny.

We have a time/space perception that allows us to track our life in a linear form. But as far as I am concerned, anything that is in your dream had already happened in your inner reality. Your dream would not show up on your mental "radar screen" if it would not be possible for you to experience it. All that is left for you to do is just to re-track the steps of how you got there. As soon as you put your attention on something, your mind starts experiencing it, and because of the mind/body connection, it gives your body sensations that match a picture or a concept in your dream. It is like when you imagine that you are sucking on a piece of lemon, you immediately feel a sour taste in your mouth.

Every time you have a dream, vision, or desire, you are already experiencing the energy of this desire moving through you. All you need is to keep noticing what you want and taking steps that make you feel good about bringing it into your physical reality it in a linear time. From this point on, your dream is already unfolding within you, and if you try to suppress it, it might become a stagnant energy that would eventually manifest itself in feelings of disappointment, depression, self-judgment, blame and resentment. People who consistently repress their dreams and desires go into emotional withdrawal from life and often have a tendency to hide in a "what's the point" state, speculating: "What would it be like if I really went for it?" It is like having a fantasy that you never fulfilled – you stay deeply connected to this experience whether you went through it or not.

I suggest that if you have an idea that inspires you, you need to put your attention on it and find resources that will help you experience this possibility. The truth of the matter is that if you have a vision, you have a blueprint of what is possible for you and all you will be doing is exploring new territory using this inner map.

Exploring the terrain is optional, but the map is always there and whether you go for it or not, you will always be curious about unexplored areas of this map. If you have the courage to go into the unknown, you might get involved in some dangerous experiences, yet after you complete your journey, you would have learned something that you did not know about yourself. Looking at the atlas does not give you that same intensity of life as the actual experience.

Just as a driver needs to decide which way to go and how to get there safe and fast, you need to make a decision which way to go in your life and what experiences to choose. Depending on your priorities, you sometimes refuse the experience and sometimes go for the whole nine yards. If you are surrounded by people who see you for who you are, they would not try to stop you from doing what you dream about. Those around you will support you and help you to be as safe as you can be while having an experience that makes a difference in your life. They would not say, "You have such a nice vehicle... Let it sit in the garage because, God forbid, something might happen to it. "

Coping With Fears

W *hat was your emotional state during my climb? How did you cope with fears for someone you love being in danger?*

Each of us has a different way to express our emotional states. When you meet someone who seems to have an "emotionless heart", this person might just be someone who does not know how to fully feel every emotion. Sometimes people are shy with their emotional self-expression or hide what they really feel behind an emotionless mask because they are afraid of being overwhelmed by it. What we call "feelings" are just the waves of energy and information that we experience with our senses. Our ability to be present with one another and be supportive of each other's experiences depends on how much emotional energy you can allow to move through your body in the moment of interaction.

When you think of something that hasn't happened yet, you are naturally creating a story that might or might not come true. Even though the story only exists in your imagination, you start experiencing an emotional reaction to that mental idea in your body. Most of the family members are worried about their climbers because there are many tragic stories out there about the high altitude expeditions. While climbers are climbing their route, their family members are creating their own notions of how dangerous it is and how their loved ones can die at any moment. These mental projections are based on what they have learned about it from the media, books and their own past experiences.

As I was observing our friends, family and even people we did not know following your expedition reports, I could see many different perceptions and stories that were created. Some were looking from a curiosity perspective, some from a perspective of really admiring what you were doing, and some were just looking for some juicy bits of information to support their fears and doubts. People really got engaged in what was happening and together we co-authored our collective narrative.

While you were pretty consistent in writing about your progress, there were other people who were also writing about your expedition. In addition, your reports coexisted with many other books, movies, and TV shows that were looked at and discussed in popular culture at the time. Some people got obsessed with tragic encounters portrayed in the media and use these stories as additional information to support their fears. Using the same information, others became even more interested and that amplified their admiration of your efforts. People's emotional response of fear or interest was nothing else but a matter of perception.

If you are familiar with the Law of Attraction that rules our progression in life, it states your vibrational quality and makes a difference in how you experience life. For example, when you focus your attention on something, your energetic frequency creates a magnet that attracts a manifestation that matches your vibration into your life. Your ability to consciously choose and direct your focus allows you to participate in your life more intentionally. If your attention is aimed at the possibility of experiencing a dangerous event, your life will be redirected accordingly. You will find many circumstances that will prove that there is always something to be fearful about. If your awareness is focused on curiosity and enthusiasm for life, you will find many different experiences that are interesting and inviting.

Every thought creates chemical elements within your body that help transmit this thought through your nervous system, so your body can produce an adequate response. When your attention is constantly projected on the person who is climbing, your fear, in my experience, affects both the person you are projecting upon, as well as yourself. If you are thinking about someone you love, do you really want to surround yourself with fear energy or reach out to them with such negative projection?

What I was doing during your climb was very nontraditional for the wife of a climber. I was watching fun movies, I was reading books unrelated to the climb, and facilitating seminars as part of my coaching service. I made a decision not to put my attention on the heaviness of the dangers and possible futility of your efforts. I focused on and therefore experienced excitement and curiosity about your trip. I knew we had done all we could to help you succeed. The rest was up to you and your dream. I made a choice to let you bring your intention into manifestation long before you went on the trip. When you were gone, my job was to stay in the present moment and trust you. I made a conscious decision to let you fully live your dream without directing your attention to my or anybody else's stories about it.

I did not feel the weight of separation because I truly believed that we were, and are, connected all the time. We all are deeply entangled with each other through our attention points, especially within the same family. This connection is strong and tangible. There is a constant energy stream between people who are close, particularly with people who have lived together for many years.

I cannot say I was completely cheerful all the time.

Of course, I experienced all kinds of discomfort. It was not an easy time for me, because there are times I have connected to everyone's worries and shared the fears of people in my environment. There were days when I was simply knocked down my emotional ladder and cried just like everybody else. At the same time, I was and I am a coach, and a healer. I knew when I was emotionally low and no longer useful to you and others. I was aware enough to know better and direct my consciousness to what was important – supporting you climbing up to the top of the world and sharing your dream and enthusiasm at all times.

What It Takes

*W*hich characteristics do you consider useful for a person who is getting ready for an Everest climb?

There are many books that are written about how to train for the extreme conditions physically. However, I believe there should be no separation between mental, emotional and physical training within your consciousness. Training usually helps you learn many ways of dealing with dangerous situations and eventually makes you so aware and attentive to the moment that you simply circumvent any of the unsafe conditions. You cannot really be mentally aware, but physically unaware. It is not about, "I am aware of my emotions, but unaware of my mental state." If you are aware, you are aware, alert and focused at every level. The rest of it cannot be called an aware state.

Unfortunately most people are unaware that they are unaware of their states in every particular moment in time. There is nothing wrong or judgmental about such general unawareness. In fact, for many of us it creates an easier, less responsible approach to life. When you are being unaware, you move along your life being occasionally surprised or struck by events that seem to be out of the norm. And if you function properly on a physical level you should feel relatively happy. You would be doing whatever you do at work – receiving bonuses, vacationing, and living happily ever after. But...

Imagine that one day you hear something or you experience something that had not been a part of your life scheme previously. Now you are aware of something that you were never aware of before. This new point of attentiveness could be anything: It could be pain in your body, or an extreme pleasure, or a concept you did not think about before. It also could be some emotional state that you did not experience prior to this moment. Once you suddenly become aware of a different reality that was not part of your life before, you start seeing things from a different perspective, and your life can never be the same.

As soon as you see something from a different perspective, you might want to explore it because now you have a curiosity (or need) that pulls you toward it. The more attention you put into exploring this new aspect of your life, the bigger connection you build with it. As you are becoming more and more aware of it, you start including this awareness into a bigger picture of your life. Because you have a different point of awareness now, everything in your life becomes colored by this awareness.

Once you have big dreams, they move you into a different state of self-awareness. In the beginning your life becomes complicated because you need time to adjust in order to make decisions that are based on your new awareness. At the same time, it simplifies your decision making process because you have a bigger picture of what you know and trust.

Together on the summit

If you have a strong desire and are committed to your evolutionary path, you will not feel content until you fulfill your dreams. Controversial opinions of the people around you should not complicate your decision. No matter what others think of you, you need to start making choices based on your personal awareness. When you began talking about the Everest climb, you started seeing everything as if through the filter of that dream. Still living an ordinary life that requires being "responsible" and "thinking through" your actions, you stepped outside of what was "normal" for everyone and accepted your own "norm".

When you asked me: "Is it a good idea to go to Mt. Everest?" my answer was, "Yes, it's an amazing idea!" Yet as you well know, there were people that said "No, it's too dangerous!" The answer to this question depended on a person's life story and was true to that individual. But could you accept their answer as your truth? You wanted something extraordinary and you found a way to achieve your dream even if others did not exactly approve of it or were not happy about your plans.

There is one more important aspect that I want to discuss here. Once you experience something grand even in a dream form, it dramatically changes you, becoming an essential part of your life. Sometimes this change creates a conflict between your goals and your family members' desires for you. The question is, "Where do you go from there?"

You would need to educate people and help them understand how you feel and what you experience while making choices that might look strange to them. At the same time, you should acknowledge the fact that even if you give them all the information in the world; they can never really know it unless they've gone through a similar experience. Coming back to your mountaineering question, people who never had their own extreme experience would probably never fully understand your drive. But even if they did, all they know is how it was for them. However, they would be able to easily relate to your big dreams. No one can know or decide for you – even me – and I went through the experience with you. Becoming aware means you are making choices that are right for you and no one else.

Making Conscious Decisions

A *ny mental / emotional preparation for big endeavors has to do with being able to ask, "Am I interested, ready and willing to take on this experience?" How do you really know that you are ready?*

First of all, most of your personal decisions are based on our collective awareness. There is a lot of information shared by people who have been there before. The danger and exhilaration of such endeavors have been vividly presented by the media, and therefore your plans might look frightening or exciting on any given day, depending on your point of observation.

Right before you went to Mt. Everest, I remember seeing Everest media products everywhere around our house: on your nightstand, in the bathroom, on the couch in the living room. Everywhere you would look, you would find the books and DVDs with those catchy names like "Into Thin Air", "Left for Dead" etc. Each of them had some sort of drama in it and I could feel it without even opening the book. My mind was being constantly bombarded by the images on the covers, directing your attention to what could happen out there. You, on the other hand, read them all and already knew what was there and having these books around was like talking to friends that just came back from the climb.

When your awareness is plugged into media, you need to understand that they have to have some sort of striking name and an impressive story in order for the book or movie to sell. Unless there is a bit of drama in every episode, and a big anticipation buildup at the end of a chapter, nobody is going to devote five to seven hours to watching the entire TV serial or read that many chapters of a book. This is also the case with the news and blogs. If the news is all about happy people going about their business who is going to watch that?

The mental preparation is about understanding these undercurrents and making a decision: "I am watching everything through the filters of my own awareness and I am not being influenced by perception of others even if they portray a lot of suffering, fears and human limitations. I choose to learn from their experience while remembering that my experience hasn't happened yet. It is up to me what it would look like.

I do not want to sound like I am diminishing anyone's heroic efforts. But sometimes a well written drama and a dynamically shot movie will amplify the drama and make it seem like climbing Everest is an impossible mission. Even though high altitude climbing is extremely dangerous, the big tragedies take place to relatively few people. But that is what people remember and that is what contributes to our collective mythology about climbing at high altitude. I truly admire everyone who explores the extraordinary and opens new horizons for those walking the dangerous paths behind them. I also want to focus our collective attention on those who successfully completed their climb while being at their peak performance, well prepared, and focused and in the flow.

I am very enthusiastic about your story, a story of someone who was well prepared, felt good, went up, and came down safely. I have a high regard for your patience with writing this book and willingness to share the details of what it takes, how to do it safely, and how to climb happily ever after.

Priorities and Responsibilities

W *hat is your view on priorities and responsibilities of someone who is going to Everest?*

This is not just a climbing question. When you are getting ready to climb a mountain such as Everest, you invest a lot of energy, time and funds into making it possible. You want to accomplish your dream, and this creates natural pressure within your life. There are also many people who know you, your plans, and maybe even support you financially. They are watching you, excited to see the result. Making your choices, you need to remember that you experience this huge collective pressure (even if you are not aware of it). This force adds additional weight to your own desire to accomplish your climbing goals and then come back home safely.

One of the most important keys to being successful in any endeavor is taking complete liability for yourself. This includes the process of making your personal distinction of success. You need to identify what a personal success means to you versus plugging into our collective understanding of how a successful person should look. For example, focusing on the pre-calculated result versus paying attention to what is unfolding in each moment of your climb can be just as dangerous as the avalanche or crevasses. To me, being a climber of Mt. Everest is not about summiting the highest mountain on Earth. It is about your ability to be true to your dreams while also being true to yourself. It is about being able to know when to say "Yes" to your aspirations and when to say "No" to your Ego.

I know that in your expedition there were people who had to turn back because they understood that they reached their personal limit and could not go any further. Some of them appreciated their time on the mountain, learned from it and left the expedition respecting both themselves and the mountain. They were successful in being fully conscious about what was happening both within and for the expedition. They were successful in completing their goals at that moment. Some of your team members came back the following year to complete their climbing aspirations. That time, with the benefit of the last years' experience, they could get all the way to the top, fulfilling their dream. There were others who kept pushing themselves beyond what was safe, even though they had numerous indications that they already reached their absolute limit. These people eventually got to the point where they had to be transported down and they stayed in a hospital bed for a long time after the trip was over.

There is no judgment and I am not talking about right or wrong decisions here. Every one of these climbers made a huge effort and followed their calling the best they could at that time. Some had accidents;

some had medical mistakes that brought these unfortunate experiences, some just felt distress seeing others injured, and dying. We can call it unpredictability at high altitude or we can look at it as a synchronicity that orchestrates the chain of events with a common denominator. Who are we to decide for others? But we definitely can decide for ourselves.

Mental and emotional training teaches you how to drop into the state of an observer and to be able to hold this state during your everyday affairs. This becomes crucial when you need to make life saving distinctions and decisions during the most extreme and challenging moments of your life.

When we talked about your goals and priorities a few months before the climb, you said that you wanted to come back safe and alive. I could feel solidity embedded in your words. You knew exactly what a successful trip would look like for you and you consciously decided to make this trip a success. I felt that you took full responsibility for your words and actions. When you finally went to Everest, your main goal was to enjoy the experience of climbing and get back home safely. I believe that this was one of the major keys to your triumphant climbing: conscious presence and responsible choices.

Awareness Training

*A*s I was training for the climb, you created a coaching program that made a difference in the consistency of my awareness. Could you please share some of your tools that helped me get ready for the Everest climb? I believe your tips *would be beneficial for those reading my book and planning their high altitude climbing training.*

Even though you were exposed to every possible danger in your Everest climb and actively participated in some of the most tragic events of the 2009 Everest chronicle, I am grateful that you did not experience the unfortunate fate of a few others. You know well how aware of your body you were before you completed my coaching program because you had a tendency to ignore all kinds of small injuries while climbing other mountains or participating in the other highly challenging activities you love.

Being an active athlete often creates a false set of objectives such as training to endure more pain then your body is ready for, ignoring minor physical problems, fatigue and a need for rest, nourishment or drink. I know that focusing on your body was not your first priority and I wanted to make sure body awareness became a good habit by the time you climbed.

Knowing that your body is not your adversary is the first step in this process. It helps you realize that if it talks to you through a subtle sensation or screams about something through pain, you should not disregard this communication. It is like listening to a friend walking up the mountain with you. If this friend is sick or in trouble, you would not ignore him or overrule his pain by saying "You should work harder!" and walk away. You do not leave your true friends behind.

Mind/body awareness is about being able to listen and respond to your body's communications before it starts screaming or completely gives up in extreme conditions of high altitude. One of my major goals in working with you as a coach was to teach you to listen to your body, notice when it was talking to you, and respond accordingly without postponing your actions.

Your specific body awareness training was a unique system that we created using many aspects of my Biofeedback, Bio-resonance and Matrix Energetics concepts which helped you notice more responses in your body, feel more relaxed and more certain. You learned that when you put your attention on your body, it talks to you and you can actually influence your mental, emotional and physical states when you know what exactly your body is asking for. For example, you were trained to create more circulation and more body/mind connection, so your extremities would not get cold even during the most freezing times of your expedition.

Inspired by my own powerful Matrix Energetics experiences, I've created supporting materials that include visual anchors and audio tracks for conscious self-reprogramming. This program facilitates inner balance and revitalizes all your systems. Listening to the guided meditations and working with different healing frequencies helped you deepen your connection to the healer within, experience a pleasure of life force flow in your organs, and learn to listen to your body's intuitive insights.

I have also created a set of positive affirmations that I embedded into a subliminal meditation CD set. Using this set helped you change an attitude toward your body. You shifted from habitually ignoring your pain and overcoming perceived weaknesses into understanding your body communications, being grateful for its cooperation and respecting its limitations. Your body awareness training assisted you in loving your body, accepting and consciously working with your level of endurance while responding to its often non-verbal communication.

This was an unfamiliar and exciting process for both of us. Our program materials created a foundation for the independent personal training that I began using with my coaching clients. They make a great support system for those wishing to find inner balance and deeper connection to their healing abilities and peak potentials. These materials are now available at **www.himalaysdream.com**

Better Safe, than Sorry

*Y*ou often emphasize an importance of awareness training in your lectures. Is there a particular connection between being in the moment and creating safety even in inherently unsafe conditions?

If you look back at your Everest experience, you would see that some of the people who became sick or injured during the climb were not 100% attentive to the seriousness of their symptoms. The warning signs showed up way before the big problem occurred, but they did not take any actions to correct their condition before it became a total disaster.

From my experience of working with hundreds of clients with post-traumatic challenges, I can attest that most people injure themselves when they are not fully present in the moment. A healthy person can check out of the moment by re-visiting past or future events up to

50 times per day. I call these "outings" mini-trances or mini self-hypnosis. When people do not value themselves, get discouraged by their work, stop paying attention to what they are doing, or can't find an understanding in their relationships, their connection to the NOW would be gone, and their presence would be gone with it.

Sometimes people simply do not want to experience low physical, emotional and mental states of boredom, anger and frustration. When you regularly experience these low consciousness states, connected to self-destructive tendencies, you attract experiences during which you might be injured, get into accidents, or experience all sorts of other misfortunes. For example, when you are a bit drunk, arguing on the phone, or tired and falling asleep behind your car wheel, it feels as if there is no-one to drive your car, yet you are still there, pretending to pay attention. This type of absence is similar to how you sometimes check out of your life, which sets the stage for trouble.

Every time you are stuck in the pain of the past or fears of the future, the life force energy is streaming past your awareness and you attract experiences that match your current emotional and mental states. When you are enjoying every moment of your unfolding life without revisiting the past or trying to hurry up the future, everything looks so vibrant, so vivid, and so alive. You become an intrinsic part of creation and you can add your effervescence to this creation. In this state you are just not in the position to attract problems.

Discovering Your Intuition

W *hat do you think is the role of intuition during high altitude climbing? Can you train yourself to be intuitive? Can you improve upon it?*

In my coaching practice I continuously meet "regular" people for whom the word "intuition" is a mystical word. A while ago, working as a corporate coach, I was even told that this word is not a good word to use in the meetings. I then decided to use the word "instinct" instead because people could connect to the idea of instinctual knowing much easier.

Intuition is often sought after as a special quality of psychics. The truth is that intuition is an ancient quality that was given to us by nature in order for us to survive. There is nothing psychic about your intuition. It starts with a sense of physical awareness. You receive an intuitive guidance from your body all the time. Intuition or instinctual knowing is linked to your physical sense of wellbeing and as such should never be overridden by your mind.

We all have this quality, and we all used it consistently as children. As we grew up and became part of the social structure, we learned that acting on our intuition was not considered appropriate all the time. So, we began suppressing our body's natural awareness and needs. Think about it, the older you get the more of your innate playful temperament and natural movement you have to hold back. You are taught to think hard and pay more attention to your thoughts than to your sensations. Without active interaction with the environment using your body wisdom, you become unaware of all the guidance available for you and start looking outside of yourself for assistance and direction.

At the same time, we cannot grow up healthy and self-sufficient without personal understanding of the mechanics of life. No one can give you your life experiences and nothing can substitute for full participation in your natural evolutionary development. Only then can you learn to listen to your bio-signals and make decisions that are true to you.

This intuitive awareness is an important step in reaching your potentials. It plays an essential role in bringing dreams into fruitful completions, guiding you to invest your energy into what has significance for you, and manage your life from the consciousness that is rooted in your present moment. Even though you might still receive other people's criticism disguised as guidance, you would be able to identify the truth that you resonate with, and make choices that protect you from relationships that are controlling or restricting your life.

Intuitive signals are not that loud. Your body will scream if you do not listen to it. In the beginning it is talking really softly. You might only feel a little inkling, but when you do, you truly have to act on it. If you are not paying attention to what your body has to say about your safety and security, eventually your body communication will grow louder. It is crucial to listen to your body's conversation and to act on your intuition BEFORE it screams with pain. Its guidance will stop you from investing your money, time, and energy in making sure that someone likes you or approves of your actions.

It will help you amplify positive outcomes of your efforts. It will also make your eyes brighter, your overall appearance more confident, and being able to command your life from a strong position of inner knowing.

Every time you dream about something, you experience your intuitive knowing talking to you about your next step. When you start wondering how it would feel if your dream came true, and use your imagination to experience more of your dream on an energetic level, your body starts having a physical experience. Your inner systems begin working to support you as if you already participate in your imaginary event. As you daydream about it, the new neuro-pathways are created and stored in your memory for the future references. If you dream a lot – and it is enjoyable – your mind and body will direct your life into bringing you more similar enjoyable experiences.

For example, I believe that your consistent dreaming about the Everest trip was exactly what brought you to the top of the world. You dreamt about creating this significant experience and all of the sudden the right people showed up in your life and you found sufficient funds needed for your expedition. Energy of people who appreciated you and your project helped you move forward from talking about your trip to actually executing it. Sometimes such support shows up as a book jumping off the shelf in the bookstore. Sometimes you receive e-mail with the information that you need. Sometimes you simply wake up feeling energized, inspired, and supported by the power of the Universe working on your behalf. Some people believe that such events are just random occurrences, some people call it synchronicity, and some call it the magic of life.

When you are open and receptive to your inner guidance, you will be positively directed by your intuitive self. You will be brought into the right place at the right time because you already experienced that through your dream and already have a sense of authenticity established through an experience of being in your dream. Your body is a great navigator. When it feels right, you just need to let go of your need to figure things out, and follow its lead.

Know Thyself

A big part of your work is connected to helping people understand their major trends and consciously use their unique characteristics to be effective in their work, safe in their environment and successful in their relationships. You helped me understand my inner authority and the life strategy that I can rely on for guidance. It was very important for me. It made a big difference in understanding of my own inklings, and it helped me make the right decisions during my climb.

Can you talk about the guidance you give people, about their energetic structure, and how it affects their life choices?

The information you are talking about comes from the genetic code of your body. When I mentor my clients, I use my extensive experience and understanding of human behaviors acquired through my study of alternative psychology and Genetic Keys. Precise calculation of each person's energetic makeup provides me with a unique blueprint of each individual's life map. It helps me interpret and communicate your behavior tendencies and interaction patterns with others. It shows how all the people in your life are connected, have a particular purpose for relating to you and a specific role in your soul's journey.

Expressed through genetic combinations, each of us has unique and powerful tools of inner evolution. Depending on your design, you have a certain strategy that supports your life script and shows you what inner communication you can trust versus what information is imposed on you by others, even if it feels like your own. Having this distinction is very useful because sensations that you can trust and sensations reflecting expectations of others are hard to differentiate. Knowing how your energy works within and how it affects others makes your decision making processes much easier. It makes you confident about your ability to understand and follow your intuitive inclinations with the right action.

I highly encourage people to explore their innate strategies, so they can change the habit of looking outside of themselves for guidance, and replace it with following inner authority and plotting their own intuitive course. Using this knowledge helps you become your own counselor. It creates a deep profound relationship with yourself that shifts you from struggling, confusion, and self–doubt into a path of self-reliance, recognition and inner freedom.

Outside Pressure or Inner Desire

I *felt that a lot of people who did not reach the top of Mt. Everest came there because they acted on somebody else's inspiration about climbing Everest. It was not really theirs. Can you share your thoughts on this?*

During our coaching sessions we talked a lot about the difference between actions based on what you desire and feel right about versus doing something out of pressure from having other people's demands. For example, most of us are taught to be initiators or leaders, but the leadership positions are not what everyone really wants. People like to be powerful, loved and successful, but for many people these feelings would not come through leadership status. Not everyone has the same level of ambitions or shares the same understanding of what it means to be successful in life. It is important to know what makes you happy and respect your true desires even if it means you live the quiet life of a gardener.

As children, we are often punished for being impulsive and following our instincts. Then we are trained to listen to more experienced and wise adults. As a result we live in mental fear that we may choose the wrong experience that might also be painful or scary. It makes us anxious about taking initiative in response to our own feelings and impulses. At the same time, nobody can give you advice that fits your purpose 100%. You are the only person who knows everything about yourself, your abilities, and your desires. Even if you think that you are unsure of what is right for you in the moment, nobody else knows as much as you do about your life.

Your Everest experience is an interesting example of how the external knowledge and your internal wisdom played the role in making the decision that was right for you. When you were getting ready for your climb, you were thinking about choosing Mt. Lhotse versus Mt. Everest because you were mentally figuring out what was right for you. You were calculating financial and physical risks involved in climbing each mountain and thought about booking both trips, so you could decide which mountain to climb later on. Everest, obviously, was emotionally more exciting, but financially more involving.

I asked you to go there and to feel into that space mentally and emotionally. I guided you into projecting yourself there and experiencing what you desired to experience in the future. This imaginary (and astral) travel helped you become clear about what you really wanted. You received the confirmation of your inner knowing that the Everest climb was exactly what you wanted. This technique eventually helped you succeed by consciously choosing the right trip, the right climbing team, and the right time frame.

You can train yourself to contemplate participation in any experience from the sensation within your body and not from your mind. With a little practice, you will notice your mind becoming just another awareness instrument, not an authority. Mental anxiety is born out of fear and pressure to survive. There is an easy way to eliminate habitual anxiety created by mentally projecting negative outcomes into the future. When you are inspired by an idea but have a fearful thought about it, put your attention down in your body. Let go of the mind struggle and feel what sensations are present when you think about your idea. Feel all your possible futures with the power of your ancient instinctual self instead of trying to analyze it with your mind.

It would really make a difference if you can allow every experience to be felt in your body, and then let your natural instincts take you there safely and in a harmonious way. Your body is the only power that can really take care of your survival. In the most challenging experiences the body simply takes over and uses all of its resources to get you out of trouble. You might help the process by consciously surrendering and accepting its wisdom before it takes over and turns on its survival mode. Talk to your body regularly so you have clear, consistent communication from within before you ever need to consult it for life and death decisions.

Mood Swings and Life Purpose

R *esting at Base Camp after my trip, I heard that some people experienced mood swings and even a state of depression after coming down from high altitudes. I did not pay much attention to this at the time. But unfortunately, I experienced the same disturbing deflating energy after my trip was over and I came back home. Can you please talk about this phenomenon?*

I am happy to address this issue because I was not only coaching you through this experience, but I was also living through the challenges it presented. You were okay for a while, but about two months after your climb, you experienced a deep state of insecurity and general disorientation in life. You were saying that you felt that your goals were achieved and there was nothing else exciting to live for. You managed to successfully come back, but you felt lost, and did not know what to do next. It was really a very challenging period in our lives. Finally, almost two years later, you become fully oriented and empowered for your next life challenges.

We had a number of conversations, trying to find your next dream, or hobby, or some sort of direction that could help you fill more engaged with life after the trip, but nothing felt right at that moment. That was a fascinating and trying phenomenon and a powerful reality check. I have also experienced this state after completing the Everest Base Camp coaching program that I offered to one of my clients just a few weeks before your trip. Coming back even from 17, 500 feet where I went, was not easy. Even though it seems not that high, it was high enough for me so that after my arrival back home, I had almost two months of extremely powerful mood swings that often left me exhausted and feeling low.

I do not really know all the mechanics of this occurrence, but what I was able to find out was connected to our brain responses to under and over oxygenation.

Coming up the trek is a long trip that is carefully focused on full acclimatization. You actually had been living at the high altitudes for two months that were needed for your brain to learn how to work with low oxygen in your system. When you were rapidly coming down, excited by your achievement and anticipating your arrival home, your brain did not have enough time to adjust to the level of oxygen at the lower altitudes. The flood of oxygen created an intense over stimulation that I believe might have contributed to your strange condition.

We both experienced a level of emotional overwhelm like never before. For me, it ranged from the deepest self-pity to the strongest expressions of anger, offense, and power mixed with the precise, almost psychic knowing of what was right for me. It really made me strong and weak at the same time. It was a very interesting feeling as I really knew what I wanted to experience in my life and was very aggressive about what I was not going to put up with any longer. It felt almost like my life acquired a different level of perspective which you can summarize with, "I've seen it from the top! Don't mess with me".

At the same time, I felt like a little baby that needed to be embraced, nurtured and loved. I needed to be taken care of, but that was not fully available to me at the time because you were gone, completing another month of your trip. I have done a lot of crying, meditating and contemplating. And I was very fortunate because I was surrounded by my apprentice team, so I had 4 – 5 people who were constantly present around me, supporting me with their loving care during that time.

I was still experiencing these mood swings when you came back. I was still going through that for a few weeks, but sometime in July I got a hold of myself. Yet, with all that I experienced, my brain did not go through your Everest extremes. Your experience was much more dramatic. So, I am not surprised that you went through it for a longer time and you are still carrying out this journey. I believe that writing this book is a great way to gather the fragments of memories and experiences that were left untouched by your awareness, so you can successfully complete your Everest story.

I also believe that your despair was only partially connected to the extreme physical challenge you experienced. Yes, you needed a longer time for fine-tuning to normal life because your level of danger and the level of adjustment were totally different from mine. The other side of the story was related to prolonged living with the higher energetic frequencies that are related to surviving at high altitudes, being exposed to superior dangers, and developing higher awareness of the world within and around you. Coming back to "normal" life, dealing with ordinary everyday tasks, and having mundane conversations did sometimes feel meaningless to me as well. The everyday "rat race" that is a part of our collective culture felt like a waste of time. Our day after day routines made no sense any longer and all that I sensed in you was a numbness and a question, "What's the point?"

At the same time, we both know that this experience elevated our life to a new level of presence. It opened up a totally new perception of what was important to you where something that you did not pay attention to before became an essential part of your life. What became really important for both of us, was learning to ask, "How would I like to experience myself now?" and really asking it enough times, so the true answer would come to us. We both trained ourselves to pay attention to our desires every time we had a feeling of low powerless or an angry emotional state, asking again and again "Is that what I want to experience? What do I want to do or not do now, so I can feel better?" and then follow up on our intuitive guidance.

Then there was a self-acknowledgement test. I remember you kept saying that summiting Everest was not a big deal for you. You felt that you were too focused on being on the task and missed the excitement of the dangerous and unknown. What you experienced after the trip was almost like self-judgment. It felt to me like you never completed your trip.

Your body was also giving you all kinds of symptoms, communicating its need to let go of the stress associated with the Mt. Everest experience as a whole. Your intuitive self was saying, "Give it a rest. Take it easy." We needed to find an outlet for easing it up and an opportunity presented itself – you were invited to share your experience with others.

As you started giving talks about your trip, sharing what you experienced in your blog, and writing this book, the magnitude of your achievement slowly started coming into your awareness. It helped you appreciate your personal skills, commitment and focus that got you to the top of the world and back home safely.

My coaching practice with you went into showing you that when you are great at achieving something, chances are you would be good at many other things. You were admitting that you had to have a high level of self-mastery in order to get up the highest mountain on Earth. You agree to trust that this same level of mastery was still there because you experienced it once, so we started looking for something you could apply your self-mastery skill to. There were tons of things that you never experienced before, so we needed to find something new to learn that would be an appropriate challenge for you, a new Everest in your life. We both shifted our attention on the teachable points of your trip that gave you a lot of confidence and a lot of positive energy toward the book, which became our next goal. Writing this book would allow you to purposefully look back, retracing every step of your journey, so your body had an opportunity to readjust through reliving a softer version of the trip and the time to recuperate.

People that undergo a huge challenge, like you, are unique, no matter how many of them are there. Sharing your experiences and relating them to other people's lives is essential and necessary for a successful completion of the integration process. I am really inspired and proud to be a part of your book. Even for me, it is almost like living through this experience again. I can only imagine what you might feel when you are revisiting these exceptional days of your life.

Blessings in Disguise

What is Next?
The trip was over, but you were at the beginning of a great adventure with new activities and resources that you did not experience before unfolding right before you. All you needed was to take a first step and feel if that was an experience you wanted.

Climbing Mt. Everest, you were receiving a lot of energy from the environment (sunlight, crisp air, beauty and freshness of every day). You learned an important survival skill of being present: to see, hear, and feel the tiniest shifts in energy. When you came back home, you had a choice of switching back to receiving energy from people, communication, and relationships which were the regular ways of energy exchange or to continue seeking for energy sources in your environment and fun activities.

It is important to remember what you have learned on the trip and being able to sustain the skill of energetic exchange that sharpened during your experience. It is essential to continue putting your attention on receiving energy from natural sources and not only from people. This adjustment re-establishes conscious connection with your energy sources that are independent of other people. I am really in awe of how you apply this imperative principal in your life now.   Even   though you were never interested in or inspired by dancing, you started dancing the Argentine Tango, the dance of connection and passion, and are very good at it.

You brought back home an amazing passion for being of service. I am astonished by your Crystal Bowls Energy Work that now is one of the new activities you enjoy sharing with people. Your sound healing group sessions are phenomenal and attract more and more people every month.

We did not know how much time it would take to complete your book project in its entirety or to feel 100% complete with this journey and its lessons. The process of writing brings a challenge of learning how to live without expectations and attachments, just as you did during your trip. But as you move on and explore life as it shows up in the now without the "big trip" coming up, you might need to surrender to the idea that nothing might ever bring you the same intensity of the moment as you experienced on the mountain. At the same time you already learned how to stay present in order to survive. You can now focus on how to intensify the pleasure hidden in very small, little things in life. You can challenge yourself with being 100% present to every experience you choose, so you can feel and appreciate the intensity in the little things that matter.

I am looking forward to the many amazing journeys and experiences that are ahead of us. I am grateful for your profound contribution in helping people to dream big and I am inspired by your message: "Be yourself! Dream big! Act on your intuition and do not ever worry about the 'How'. You can be, do or have what you want in life, even without quitting your day job!"

45005954R00126

Made in the USA
Lexington, KY
15 September 2015